D0875826

WITHDRAWN

A MATTER OF COMFORT

IMMIGRANT COMMUNITIES & ETHNIC MINORITIES IN THE UNITED STATES & CANADA: No. 32

ISSN 0749-5951

Series Editor: Robert J. Theodoratus
Department of Anthropology, Colorado State University

1. James G. Chadney. *The Sikhs of Vancouver.*
2. Paul Driben. *We Are Metis: The Ethnography of a Halfbreed Community in Northern Alberta.*
3. A. Michael Colfer. *Morality, Kindred, and Ethnic Boundary: A Study of the Oregon Old Believers.*
4. Nanciellen Davis. *Ethnicity and Ethnic Group Persistance in an Acadian Village in Maritime Canada.*
5. Juli Ellen Skansie. *Death Is for All: Death and Death-Related Beliefs of Rural Spanish-Americans.*
6. Robert Mark Kamen. *Growing Up Hasidic: Education and Socialization in the Bobover Hasidic Community.*
7. Liucija Baskauskas. *An Urban Enclave: Lithuanian Refugees in Los Angeles.*
8. Manuel Alers-Montalvo. *The Puerto Rican Migrants of New York City.*
9. Wayne Wheeler. *An Analysis of Social Change in a Swedish-Immigrant Community: The Case of Lindsborg, Kansas.*
10. Edwin B. Almirol. *Ethnic Identity and Social Negotiation: A Study of a Filipino Community in California.*
11. Stanford Neil Gerber. *Russkoya Celo: The Ethnography of a Russian-American Community.*
12. Peter Paul Jonitis. *The Acculturation of the Lithuanians of Chester, Pennsylvania.*
13. Irene Isabel Blea. *Bessemer: A Sociological Perspective of a Chicano Bario.*
14. Dorothy Ann Gilbert. *Recent Portuguese Immigrants to Fall River, Massachusetts: An Analysis of Relative Economic Success.*
15. Jeffrey Lynn Eighmy. *Mennonite Architecture: Diachronic Evidence for Rapid Diffusion in Rural Communities.*
16. Elizabeth Kathleen Briody. *Household Labor Patterns among Mexican Americans in South Texas: Buscando Trabajo Seguro.*
17. Karen L. S. Muir. *The Strongest Part of the Family: A Study of Lao Refugee Women in Columbus, Ohio.*
18. Judith A. Nagate. *Continuity and Change Among the Old Order Amish of Illinois.*
19. Mary G. Harris. *Cholas: Latino Girls and Gangs.*
20. Rebecca B. Aiken. *Montreal Chinese Property Ownership and Occupational Change, 1881—1981.*
21. Peter Vasiliadis. *Dangerous Truths: Interethnic Competition in a Northeastern Ontario Goldmining Community.*
22. Bruce La Brack. *The Sikhs of Northern California, 1904—1975: A Socio—Historical Study.*
23. Jenny K. Phillips. *Symbol, Myth, and Rhetoric: The Politics of Culture in an Armenian-American Population.*
24. Stacy G. H. Yap. *Gather Your Strength, Sisters: The Emerging Role of Chinese Women Community Workers.*
25. Phyllis Cancilla Martinelli. *Ethnicity In The Sunbelt: Italian-American Migrants in Scottsdale, Arizona.*
26. Dennis L. Nagi. *The Albanian-American Odyssey: A Pilot Study of the Albanian Community of Boston, Massachusetts.*
27. Shirley Ewart. *Cornish Mining Families of Grass Valley, California.*
28. Marilyn Preheim Rose. *On the Move: A Study of Migration and Ethnic Persistence among Mennonites from East Freeman, South Dakota.*
29. Richard H. Thompson. *Toronto's Chinatown: The Changing Social Organization of an Ethnic Community.*
30. Bernard Wong. *Patronage, Brokerage, Entrepreneurship and the Chinese Community of New York.*

Continued at back of book

A MATTER OF COMFORT

Ethnic Maintenance and Ethnic Style among Third-Generation Japanese Americans

Kaoru Oguri Kendis

AMS Press, Inc.
New York

Library of Congress Cataloging-in-Publication Data

Kendis, Kaoru Oguri.
A matter of comfort : ethnic maintenance and ethnic style among third-generation Japanese Americans / by Kaoru Oguri Kendis.
p. cm. — (Immigrant communities & ethnic minorities in the United States & Canada ; 32)
Bibliography: p.
Includes index.
ISBN 0-404-19442-7
1. Japanese Americans—Ethnic identity. 2. Ethnicity—United States. 3. Japanese Americans—Cultural assimilation. I. Title. II. Series.
E184.J3K45 1989
305.8'956'073—dc19 88-36700
CIP

All AMS books are printed on acid-free paper that meets the guidelines for performance and durability of the Committee on Production Guidelines for Book Longevity of the Council on Library Resources.

AMS PRESS
56 East 13th Street
New York, N.Y. 10003, U.S.A.

MANUFACTURED IN THE UNITED STATES OF AMERICA

DEDICATION

To my husband, Randall, who made it possible to finish this, and

To our children

Daniel Yukio
David Tokuzo
Adam Takezo

who made it almost impossible.

TABLE OF CONTENTS

ACKNOWLEDGMENTS

The number of people who contributed to the completion of this work is surprisingly large, and the method the author has to acknowledge the debt to them surprisingly meager. To merely thank them in this acknowledgment does not do justice to roles they have played, and hopefully each will recognize that my gratitude goes deeper than the words on this page.

First, and most importantly, thanks is due to those individuals who opened themselves to me so that I could look in. Given the value that many place on privacy and the tendency Japanese Americans have to avoid expressing their feelings and disclosing personal information except to the closest friends, this was difficult for some. Without their help and forbearance this study would never have been possible.

Next I would like to thank my parents, Mikihiko and Marjorie Oguri, for their support and encouragement over the many years it took me to reach this point. Their open-minded approach to life and firm commitment that people are people regardless of individual culture, social, racial or religious differences undoubtedly played a role in shaping my own attitudes.

Credit is also due to L. Keith Brown, Gary Allison, Leonard Plotnicov, Ian Rawson, Richard Scaglion, Alexander Spoehr and Allen Tan who provided many useful comments, suggestions and criticisms.

I would like to express my thanks to my husband, Randall Kendis, who while conducting his own research, shared the ups-and-downs of my research experience. Without his help through each stage of the research - from arguing method and theory, helping with data analysis, word processing, etc. – the project would have been considerably more difficult.

And finally, a "thank you" to my sister, Chiyomi Wellington-Oguri, who put in considerable time, thought and energy in helping to edit this work.

INTRODUCTION

Current research on ethnicity in culturally plural societies has focused attention on the loss of ethnic identity and the eventual assimilation of ethnic groups into mainstream society, or on the strategic use of some aspect of ethnicity to increase access to some valued but scarce resource and hence facilitate survival in a new society.

Among Japanese Americans ethnicity has persisted into the third and fourth generations. It is not a stage through which they are passing on their way to assimilation. Instead, the ethnic identity of these individuals is a focal point around which important realms of their lives are organized. Using even the most superficial definition of ethnicity, this is evident in wide-based social and institutional networks which are exclusive of nonJapanese Americans.

Nor is ethnicity a scheme for their survival. As a group, Japanese Americans are well-educated, economically successful and socially accepted. They are found comfortable in the middle and upper-middle classes, face no apparent discrimination and seem to be well assimilated into American society. Organizing on the basis of ethnic category does not alter their economic or political position, nor is it a strategy employed to improve access to scarce resources. Prejudice is the infrequent exception and discrimination does not provide a strong impetus for defensively banding together and does not prevent them from participating fully in American life.

The obvious question arises: Why does ethnicity continue to remain salient for these third- and fourth-generation Japanese Americans? More generally, why does ethnicity continue to be significant for later generations of former immigrant groups? Given the why, the focus then shifts to the how: How is ethnicity developed, and how is it maintained?; how does one "become" ethnic?

THE WHAT OF ETHNICITY - AN OPERATIONAL DEFINITION

Before discussing the why and how, we must first define the "what" of ethnicity. Much of current research has devalued the term "ethnic" through its indiscriminate use in labeling anything or anyone of a cultural, geographic or racial origin different from that of the person doing the labeling. An operational definition of ethnicity is needed to re-establish it as a tool of analytic value.

As understood here, ethnicity is composed of two necessary elements - the psychological or internal aspect, and the behavioral or external aspect.

The psychological aspect of ethnicity is the self identification of an individual in a plural society with a group of the same cultural origin as his own. Inherent in this identification is his recognition that his group is different in meaningful ways from other groups of the same order in the society and that these differences ultimately stem from differences in cultural heritage.

The behavioral aspect is his use, whether consciously or unconsciously, of elements of his ethnic culture to identify himself as a member of the group. These elements may be the more easily observable aspects such as language or style of dress, or more subtle, such as proper social behavior. These elements need not be identical to those of the culture of origin; the ethnic culture is dynamic and adapting, and may be quite different from the culture of the nation of origin.

As here defined, ethnicity is not a yes/no affair, but can be expressed as a continuum. Individuals can identify in varying degrees with their ethnic group and can be more or less conforming in behavior. Hence, individuals can be high ethnic, low ethnic or somewhere in between.

This definition varies somewhat from current usage in its requirement of both a psychological/individual element and a behavioral/social element within a cultural context. Some scholars regard psychological identification as of singular importance in ethnicity. De Vos (1975) states that ethnicity is determined by what a person feels about himself and not by how he is observed to behave. We have found, however, that a display of behavior defined as ethnic by the ethnic group is equally important. Belief may give an individual the potential for becoming ethnic but there must also be some sort of observable, agreed upon behavior in order to be ethnic, in order to activate that potential for ethnicity. When a Japanese American does not follow the rules of social behavior deemed necessary for being a "real" Japanese American, he is not accepted as one, regardless of his psychological identification. High ethnic *sansei* call Japanese Americans who lack the proper behavior "bananas" - a derogatory term - meaning yellow on the outside, but white on the inside. Some observable, agreed upon behavior is necessary for ethnicity to exist. Ethnicity cannot exist as an individual phenomenon but must involve some interaction between fellow ethnics. Hence ethnicity is simultaneously cultural, social and psychological.

Markers exist which channel and pattern relationships and behavior within and between groups (Barth 1969). If these markers are seen by the actors as ultimately arising from differences in culture or cultural ancestry, they may serve as ethnic markers. The markers do not have to be of a specific type (e.g., language or dress) to mark ethnic boundaries; they need only to be believed by the ethnic members themselves to have developed or evolved from their cultural heritage, whatever the content of the marker may be. Furthermore, it is not one specific marker or trait that makes an individual ethnic or not to members of the ethnic group. Rather, it consists of varieties and clusters of traits that make this difference between high ethnic and a low ethnic and between an insider and an outsider. The symbols or markers of ethnic identity and boundaries undergo change from generation to generation, and may assume forms that to a previous generation were not seen as ethnic markers (e.g., Schildkrout 1974). Thus, first- and second-generation Japanese Americans may view the third-generation as totally American, i.e., completely Americanized, even though the high ethnic members of this later generation continue to draw boundaries to distinguish themselves from others. These markers they believe to be the result of cultural differences.

In order for a person to be ethnic he must both identify himself as ethnic and be accepted by the ethnic group as such. Various factors in an individual's life may act as pressures towards ethnicity, without being causes in themselves. Discrimination by outsiders may "encourage" one to become a member of an ethnic group but it is not in itself a determining factor. Hence, ascription of an individual to an ethnic category is of secondary importance (c.f. Barth 1969; Dirks 1975).

The biological fact of birth to parents with a different cultural heritage, and the sociological fact of initial socialization in a different cultural environment are also insufficient to determine ethnicity. Many third-generation Japanese Americans are proud of their Japanese ancestry and enjoy observing some Japanese or Japanese American customs. However, they do not want to organize their entire social lives around this ancestry. Aside from a few differences that they consider minor, they do not see themselves as significantly different from the generality of Americans. They prefer not to divide their world into two discrete categories - Japanese American and nonJapanese American - and see no inherent advantages in interacting mainly with Japanese Americans. Despite their birth and upbringing, they are low ethnics.

THE WHY OF ETHNICITY

In the light of this definition, we can examine the benefits of ethnicity for Japanese Americans, in particular for the later generations.

The advantages of ethnicity for immigrants to a new culture are clear. Ethnic identification provides a degree of psychological comfort and, in the case of the Japanese immigrants, some assurance of economic aid from their fellow "ethnics" in times of need. The continuation of ethnic behavior results in the "re-creation in miniature" of the more familiar life of the mother country, and thus, in a more manageable life.

The third- and fourth-generation Japanese Americans, however, are in a much different position than their new immigrant ancestors. They are well educated within the American school system, economically advantaged, socially accepted and highly acculturated. In fact, they are widely regarded as one of the most successful groups of recent immigrant origin in both their rapid acculturation and socioeconomic success.

In addition, the Japanese American ethnic community has undergone extreme internal and external dislocation and disruption. With the outbreak of war between the United States and Japan, all persons of Japanese ancestry living on the West Coast (the majority of Japanese Americans) were suddenly incarcerated in relocation camps or forced to relocate elsewhere in the country. At the camps, they were forced to make a formal identification with either Japan or America, for use by the government in determining their future in America.

Despite the results of this dislocation - the disruption of pre-war ethnic organizations, the more-or-less successful destruction of Japanese identity, the weakening of family life due to the structure of the camps, the rapid acculturation of the second-generation - and despite their post-war success in the larger society, many Japanese Americans maintain their ethnicity today, albeit in a different form than that of their parents and grandparents.

The answer to <u>why</u> ethnicity endures among these Japanese Americans lies, ultimately, in cultural differences. Despite their high level of acculturation and the intermeshing of most aspects of their lives into American society, high ethnic Japanese Americans find significant differences between their own ways of interaction and those of the larger society. These differences are not the readily observable cultural elements of language, food or dress, but the more subtle and deeply rooted values, attitudes and behavior patterns, which result in particular forms of interpersonal relations. These differences manifest themselves in a <u>sense of comfort</u> which high ethnic Japanese Americans feel when interacting with others like themselves, deriving from a shared style of interaction distinctive from those found in the larger outside society.

To the outsider, these differences many seem insignificant, but they constitute <u>the</u> primary reason high ethnic Japanese Americans have for partitioning the social segment of their lives and limiting access to it almost solely to other Japanese Americans. The instrumental aspects of their lives - making a living, getting an education, taking part in the political system - are intermeshed with mainstream society. They choose, however, to act out the more personally meaningful and satisfying non-instrumental portions of their lives with other Japanese Americans. They do so, moreover, in such a way as to practically exclude nonJapanese Americans.

High ethnic Japanese Americans place a strong value on their ethnic style, viewing it as superior to that of the outside society.

This value is often reinforced by acculturation in a racially exclusive environment. In addition, the rules governing their behavior in these more personal portions of their lives are often in conflict with those of nonJapanese Americans. High ethnic Japanese Americans tend to feel at a disadvantage dealing with outsiders who live by different rules. Conversely, they feel comfortable interacting with Japanese Americans who share their standards and with whom they may have more "natural" relationships.

THE HOW OF ETHNICITY

Given that these Japanese Americans are so immersed in society outside their ethnic group, what mechanisms and structures make it possible for them to keep one portion of their lives exclusively Japanese American? We have found friendship networks, ethnically-based organizations and a system of reciprocal obligation to be agents in facilitating communication and interaction between Japanese Americans. Simultaneously, they effectively limit social interaction with nonJapanese Americans. They also provide opportunities for the children of high ethnic parents to learn the subtle but significant configuration of values, attitudes and behaviors which constitute the patterned "ethnic style."

The remainder of this work is designed around the framework of the WHAT, WHY and HOW of ethnicity in the specific case of our Japanese American sample. The <u>what</u> is as much a statement of theoretical position as it is an operational one, and how it was arrived at is covered in Chapter 2 - METHODOLOGY, along with the method by which "high ethnics" and "low ethnics" were delineated. An analysis of the significant differences appearing between "high" and "low" ethnic third- and fourth-generation Japanese Americans is addressed in Chapter 4 - DIFFERENCES BETWEEN HIGH ETHNICS

AND LOW ETHNICS. In the interest of readability, recitation of specific statistical tests utilized and their numerical results are kept to a minimum throughout the text, and summary tables can be found in Appendix A.

The why of ethnicity in this case is dealt with primarily in Chapters 3 and 5. Chapter 3 - HISTORY AND SETTING - gives an overview of the rather trying road that the Japanese Americans have tread to bring them to where they are today. Chapter 5 - WHY DOES ETHNICITY PERSIST FOR LATER GENERATIONS? - delves into the specific elements found in the research to account for the manifestation and persistence of ethnicity, among them cultural differences and ethnic style.

The how of ethnicity is analyzed and discussed in Chapters 6, 7 and 8. Based upon the quantitative data, these chapters together provide a more qualitative discussion of how one "becomes" a high or low ethnic, what mechanisms and structures have been developed and exist to maintain ethnicity, and how these elements may differ with other variables such as residential location (Chapter 7 - ETHNICITY IN THE SUBURBS).

This work is written in the present tense, to reflect what is commonly referred to as the "ethnographic present", in this case July, 1977 through August, 1978.

METHODOLOGY

Over a 13 month period, from mid-July, 1977, through August of 1978, I resided in the city of Gardena, in Los Angeles county, California. Gardena's population included a high concentration of Japanese Americans and a substantial number of Japanese nationals. In addition, the Japanese American community was very active.

The original intent was to concentrate on this single community, but the research was soon expanded to include Japanese Americans living in the more suburban environment of Orange county.

Although not economically homogeneous, Gardena tended to be a working and solid middle class community. By contrast, the new suburbs of Orange county had attracted many young, upper-middle class Japanese American families. By thus including a wider range of socioeconomic levels in the sample, I hoped to explore the contention that ethnicity is found only among people of lower socioeconomic background (e.g., Dirks 1975; Ebuchi 1971; Greer 1974; Levine & Montero 1973) while those more educated and socially and economically successful assimilate into the mainstream culture.

In addition, Gardena was a city with strong residential concentrations of Japanese Americans; in Orange county, the Japanese Americans were scattered. I was thus able to compare the effects of the differing residential patterns on ethnicity.

I used a combination of individually administered questionnaire, formal interview and the traditional anthropological technique of participant-observation. The research period consisted of three phases. Phase 1 (2½ months) was spent becoming generally familiar with the Gardena Japanese American community and an ethnic church in Orange county, establishing contacts with people in both areas and developing an appropriate questionnaire. During phase 2 (about 4 months) I administered the questionnaire (Appendix B) to 102 individuals. A computer analysis of the resultant data enabled me to select a subset of the original sample for intensive interviewing. Phase 3 (6½ months) was devoted to these interviews. Throughout all three phases data was gathered through observation of, and participation in, community life and activities and through informal interviews and conversations with community members.

PHASE 1

The difficulty that anthropologists have had in establishing rapport with groups under study is well documented. These difficulties are compounded in the modern urban environment. The numbers of people and institutions are great, lives are highly complex and segmented and there is no single commonly shared institution or person to serve as a stage for introduction.

I had anticipated these difficulties in the abstract. I was caught unawares, however, by the extreme initial reserve of Japanese Americans with strangers, especially strangers asking questions. Furthermore, Gardena was convenient to a number of colleges and universities and was known as an area of high Japanese American concentration; each term, numerous researchers and students passed out questionnaires for research and term papers. As a result, there was a growing antipathy towards being studied, particularly on the part of community leaders and especially because there was no apparent benefit to themselves.

Consequently, I had great difficulty getting to know people on an informal basis. An important breakthrough was made by attending classes at the Gardena Valley Japanese Cultural Institute. The shared activity facilitated informal conversation and the development of casual relationships with classmates. At the same time, I attended a Japanese American ethnic church in Orange county and gradually became familiar with members of the congregation. Also several Japanese American community workers were helpful in their willingness to talk and make suggestion.

During the latter part of this phase, I developed a questionnaire and revised it with the help of several community members. A major purpose of the questionnaire was to provide an objective index of the degree of ethnicity of each individual in order to select high and low ethnics for intensive interviewing. Questions were developed to explore both the psychological and behavioral identity of the respondent.

The questionnaire was quite long, necessitated by the premise that no single element, but rather an individual combination of factors makes a person a high or low ethnic. Since the questionnaire was to be computer analyzed, questions were primarily close-ended.

PHASE 2

A total of 102 third- and fourth-generation Japanese Americans answered the questionnaire. The sample was opportunistic and not random; respondents were reached by referrals from another respondent. The minimum criteria for an interviewee were that he be third- or fourth-generation and have completed his education. A range of education and income levels and both single and married people were included.

The sample consisted of 39 males and 63 females. Their ages ranged from 18 to 46 with the average being about 30. Over half were married. All of them had at least finished high school. The majority (about 65%) had a college degree or higher. Annual incomes ranged from none (unemployed) to well over $40,000. Over two-thirds were Christian. The rest were Buddhist, belonged to some other religious sect or had no religious affiliation.

Each questionnaire was personally administered; questionnaire sessions usually took place in the informant's home and lasted about 1 to 2 hours. While more time consuming than a mailed questionnaire and limiting the sample size, this approach had several important advantages. Researchers had found a low return rate for mailed surveys of Japanese Americans; personally filling out the questionnaire with each individual ensured it would be completed. Long informal conversations frequently resulted from the personal contact, enabling me to gather more data than just that elicited by the questionnaire. More importantly, it gave each interviewee an opportunity to know me better and become more involved in the research, thereby increasing the probability that those selected would be willing to take the time for further intensive interviewing.

The questions fell in six categories: those dealing with 1) the psychological identification of the respondent; 2) his activities and behavior; 3) his perception of being different as a Japanese American; 4) the importance he placed on passing on the heritage to his children; 5) the prejudice he had experienced and perceived; and 6) personal information and otherwise uncategorized questions. Answers were in the form of numbers from 1 to 4 reflecting how strongly the person felt about a particular subject - the higher number indicating the stronger feeling. Respondents' answers in each of the categories 1 through 5 were summed; hence each person had five derived category scores. The top and bottom 25% (approximately)[1] of each index were isolated. Item analysis was used to determine whether the individual items in the index successfully distinguished between the top and bottom groups.[2] In this way the questions which did not significantly distinguish between high and low scores in the category were eliminated.

The prejudice category proved of little significance overall and was dropped from further analysis.

After the elimination of insignificant items, each person's totals were recomputed for categories 1 through 4. The inter-index correlation coefficients (Table 1) all reached a significant level. They were generally moderate to strong, supporting the assertion that while the indexes were related, they measured separate factors.

Total scores for each category were standardized (z scores) so that each category was equally weighted. The sum of the categories 1 through 4 was the Total Ethnic Score of each respondent. Individuals were then ranked based on this composite score.

PHASE 3

Twenty-eight individuals were selected from the top and bottom 25% of the rank-ordered informants for further interviewing. Research subjects were chosen who were willing to be further questioned, who seemed to be good informants and who, taken as a group, reflected a range of income and marital statuses. This smaller sample included 13 low ethnics and 15 high ethnics. One-third were male and over half were married. Most had children.

Interviewing usually took place in the homes of the individuals. The interviews often involved several sessions. A single interview might be concluded in a four to five hour visit or might run for as many as six sessions. The average was about three sessions.

The interviewing was initially based on the questionnaire. All the close-ended questions became open-ended; other topics of interest were explored as they arose. Life histories of the informants were also collected.

Throughout phase 3, I continued to collect information from people encountered after the questionnaires had been administered. Participation in and observation of community activities also continued.

TABLE 1

CORRELATION MATRIX OF INDICES

	1	2	3	4	5
Importance of Passing on Heritage (1)	1.0000	.6664	.5267	.6253	.8654
Psychological Identification (2)		1.0000	.6236	.5112	.8384
Perception of Differences (3)			1.0000	.4893	.7872
Activities & Behavior (4)				1.0000	.7704
Total Ethnic Score (5)					1.0000

Pearson product moment correlation coefficients. All correlations were significant at the $p \leq .001$ level.

HISTORY AND SETTING

JAPANESE IN AMERICA

The history of Japanese immigration to America is a relatively short one - little more than one hundred years. For over two centuries, no Japanese were allowed to leave Japan by decree of the ruling military government. In 1854, Commodore Perry forced the government to reopen the country and Japanese could emigrate to other countries. Initially only the upper classes and students were permitted abroad. In 1884, the laboring classes, who formed the bulk of the settlers in America, were allowed to emigrate and came as contract laborers for Hawaiian sugar plantations (Ichihashi 1932:6). Eventually other Japanese of the laboring class (mostly farmers) reached the mainland United States, either directly from Japan or via Hawaii once their contracts were completed.

The *Issei* - Early Days in America

Between 1890 and 1940 only about 200,000 Japanese immigrated to the U.S. The total U.S. immigration during that period was 25 million; yet to many Americans, it seemed as if a yellow horde was descending. The Japanese were a physically visible population often in a region with a history of anti-Chinese sentiment. They tended to concentrate in a relatively few geographic areas and in a narrow range of occupations. By 1940, 75% of the mainland Japanese had settled in California More than half were in six counties where they tended to cluster in enclaves, both in the urban and rural areas

(Daniels 1972:78-79). Initially most immigrants worked as seasonal laborers in railroading, logging and lumbering, fishing and farming. In later years many turned to farming, first as migrant laborers, then as sharecroppers and tenant farmers (Thomas 1952:21). In the urban areas they generally worked as domestic workers, gardeners, or shopkeepers serving the ethnic community or specializing in a few activities catering to the general public (Thomas 1952:27).

The early immigrants were overwhelmingly single males. Many were second and third sons ineligible by primogeniture to inherit any of their family's holdings. Like so many immigrants before them,they had come intending to make their fortunes and return to Japan as rich men. Few came with the intention of permanently settling here. However, as the years passed, the immigrants gained some measure of economic stability but except for a very few, no great fortune. In the early 1900s, realizing their stay would be longer than expected, they sent back to Japan for picture brides.

This was also a period of rising anti-Asian and anti-Japanese sentiment on the Pacific coast. A number of restrictive laws against the Japanese were passed. One such law was the Webb-Heney Act of 1913 which declared that Japanese aliens could not legally buy land or hold leases for more than three years. Another was the Immigration Act of 1924 which ended further Japanese immigration to America.

Despite the growing restrictions the Japanese found ways to legally circumvent many of them. Rather than displacing previously established farmers, the *issei* farmers, often opened up new farmland, such as the Imperial Valley in California. They were very successful with their labor intensive, high yield style of agriculture as opposed to the resource intensive methods of American farming. In 1919, they held about 1% of California farmland under cultivation, but the market value of their crops was over 10% of the dollar value of California agriculture (Daniels 1972:86). In the production of many important truck crops they had obtained virtual monopolies. They produced 30-35% by value of all commercial truck crops grown in California (Thomas 1952:25).

In the urban sector, the Japanese flourished in some businesses - especially in the wholesale and retail sale of agricultural products. By 1939, there were 149 Japanese-operated wholesale establishments listed in Los Angeles. In 1941, they were estimated to have handled more than 60% of the total amount of business, grossing an estimated $26,500,000 (Thomas 1952:36).

The *Nisei* - Pre-World War II

The offspring of these immigrants, the *nisei*, were American citizens by right of birth. They were far more educated than their parents. Many had a college education. Although the *nisei* did well economically, most found it difficult to break out of the ethnic community for better opportunities. There was continuing anti-Japanese discrimination from the outside and pressure for ethnic solidarity from the inside.

In one study of *nisei* male college graduates who entered the labor force before World War II, only 10% of the sample found professional jobs. Only 20% secured managerial jobs, although this figure included farm enterprises, often their family's. Of the *nisei* who went on to do graduate study, only 48% were able to enter the professional ranks immediately (Levine and Montero 1973:44). Since it was extremely difficult to succeed outside the ethnic community, many *nisei* had to remain within the community and under the authority of their parents. It was quite common for young men with a college degree to take jobs as salesmen, fruitstand attendants and vegetable washers (Kitano 1969:49).

World War II and Relocation

Antagonism towards the Japanese in America reached a new peak on December 7, 1941 with the attack on Pearl Harbor by Japan. On January 29, 1942, all enemy aliens (meaning all Japanese immigrants, since they were not allowed to become citizens) were required to leave the Pacific coast by the U.S. government. Few, however, were able to relocate due to the hostility they encountered when they attempted to enter other states. In March of 1942, all persons of Japanese ancestry - foreign-born and American citizens alike - were ordered to concentration camps under the aegis of the War Relocation Authority (WRA). In most cases, the evicted people had only one week's notice of their removal. Some had as little as 48 hours in which to sell, rent, loan, store or give away property and possessions. Administrative defects and the circumstances of the Japanese American population made losses inevitable for even the most sophisticated of businessmen. The majority of the population was not equipped to deal with the situation; many were economically destroyed.

The American camps were not meant to be a means of punishment but camp life was grim and institutional. Even more, it substantially loosened family bonds. Families were assigned one or two rooms in drafty barracks. Only communal toilets and showers were available. Meals were eaten in cafeterias. Families no longer gathered together at meals and people did their best to stay away from the unpleasant housing, using them only as places to sleep.

Along with the severe disruption of the community and of family life, formal policy of the WRA encouraged a total adherence to "American" ways. The camp community was as nearly as possible to conform with American practice in its outlook and organization. Only U.S. citizens could vote and hold office in the camp government. By federal legislation the *issei* could not become naturalized citizens. The effect of this ruling was to remove power from the parents who traditionally held it and place it in the hands of their offspring. Also, the director of the WRA gave special preference to the *nisei*, since he felt they would help to Americanize the imprisoned community (Broom and Kitsuse 1956).

The original goal of the WRA was not permanent incarceration, but rather relocation to areas of the country where there was no history of organized anti-Asian sentiment. It was not a total success, however. Many people, particularly the *issei*, were unable or unwilling to leave the camps and start over again elsewhere.

The camps did not begin to close until January, 1945, when the West Coast mass exclusion order was rescinded. It was an uncertain period for most Japanese Americans. Many were afraid to return to their former homes on the Pacific coast. Some chose to resettle in other parts of the country where they hoped for a more cordial reception. Still, many of them did return. As the years passed many more continued to return until once again the highest concentration of Japanese Americans outside of Hawaii was on the West coast. As before the war, they tended to cluster in particular counties and cities.

The Post-World War II Japanese American Community

The *issei* returned from the camps to find their businesses gone. Many were able to re-establish themselves, but others were too old or too discouraged to begin the struggle again. The Japanese business communities never regained their pre-war levels of activity.

The *nisei*, the second-generation, however, found new opportunities open to them that by their education they were prepared to take. Rather than filling the gaps left in the ethnic community by the first-generation, many preferred to leave and seek professional work or salaried and wage positions in the employ of others (Miyamoto 1972:239). Levine and Montero Japanese American male college graduates who entered the job market in the post-war period from 1946 to 1952; 55% obtained high status jobs, 48% being in the professional ranks (versus 10% in the pre-war period). Of another 10% who did graduate work, 70% became professional (1973:44). In California, nearly one-half of the Japanese American population had been involved in farming. In 1960, less than one-third were still involved, whereas more than 38% were in professional, technical and white-collar fields (Daniels 1972:86).

The years following the war had generally been good ones economically for the *nisei* and their offspring. Many had made it into middle class security and were seen by the outside society as a "model minority" who succeeded in American society. This had been done this in the space of two generations and without the violence and confrontation tactics of other minority groups. In a study done by Schmid and Nobbe, based on the 1960 census, it was shown that the Japanese population in America had a greater percentage of college graduates than the white population (18.4% Japanese vs. 10.3% white). The had a greater percentage of its people in white collar occupations (56.0% Japanese vs. 42.1% white). They were second only to white males in terms of median income (the median income for Japanese males was 99.3% of the median income of white males) (1965:913-919). This ethnic group had done so well, that people both within and outside the ethnic community felt that the third-generation was, in everything except appearance, white.

THE SETTING: GARDENA

At the time of this research, Gardena, was a city of over five square miles with a population of approximately 46,000. It lay about fifteen miles south of metropolitan Los Angeles in Los Angeles county. It is land locked and surrounded by other communities in various stages of development (Soo Hoo 1974).

It was originally part of the great rancho estates of the Dominguez, Amestoy, Ducazau and Rosecrans families. The rich soil conditions and plentiful water supply attracted a number of ranchers and farmers. Around 1900, Japanese immigrants began to farm in the area, growing flowers, vegetables and strawberries. The Gardena Valley area soon became the strawberry growing center of Southern California.

Gardena officially became a city in 1930, when it incorporated with the neighboring communities of Moneta, Western City and Strawberry Park.

The number of Japanese families in this farming community grew slowly but steadily until the beginning of World War II. With the closing of the relocation camps, many of the pre-war residents, joined by newcomers, settled again in the Gardena Valley. Various Japanese American community organizations were reactivated and reorganized and new ones came into existence.

From a heavily farming community Gardena had evolved into a residential suburb supported by small business and both light and heavy industry. At the time of this research, there were no longer any farms although there were a number of nurseries. Gardena also had legalized gambling which attracted Southern California residents and tourists. Through taxes and good will contributions they have been a good source of income for the city.

In the post-war years, Gardena was one of the communities that attracted *nisei* who had reached the relative affluence of the middle class. Consequently their third-generation offspring were seen as spoiled and snobbish by their peers who had remained in the poorer sections of Los Angeles .

The 9,144 residents of Japanese ancestry represent 21.1% of Garden's population. In 1978, Gardena was the city with the highest concentration of Japanese on the mainland United States. This percentage includes the *shosha*, Japanese nationals who had been sent by their companies to work for a number of years in America.

Gardena was a community undergoing change. Black residents had increased from 3.6% of the population in 1970 to 21.9% in 1978. The white population had decreased 56.7% of the community in 1970 to 35.7% in 1978. The fourth largest group, the Hispanic had remained fairly stable in size. With the growing influx of blacks, the more affluent members of the community - particularly the white and Japanese American elements - had begun to move into neighboring areas that were still heavily white, or into the new suburbs of Orange county. There was still a large body of Japanese American residents. The percentage of Japanese residents had remained stable, however, only because it was bolstered by the increasing number of *shosha* employees and their families.

Although it comprised about a fifth of the Gardena's population in 1978, the Japanese population appeared to be much larger for a number of reasons. The Japanese tended to cluster residentially in certain areas, particularly southern Gardena. There were entire blocks containing nearly all Japanese families. This residential clustering led to the concentration of Japanese American students in particular schools. There were nine elementary schools but most of the Asian students were found in only two (Gaines 1976:5).

Japanese Americans, and Japanese nationals played a highly visible political role. Gardena operated under the City Council - Administrative Officer form of government; of its four councilmen, two were Japanese American. The city treasurer was Japanese American and the previous mayor was Japanese American. Many of the small businesses were Japanese American owned. These businesses ran the range from the generalized American type drugstores, beauty parlors, service stations, etc. to the more noticeably ethnic Japanese restaurants, gift shops, confectioneries, bonsai nurseries, etc. There was even one shopping center which consisted of shops selling Japanese merchandise and/or are Japanese operated. Of the six banks in Gardena, three were Japanese and there was a Japanese credit union.

There were a number of churches whose congregations were almost exclusively Japanese American or Japanese. These churches tended to be large and housed in Japanese styled buildings.

There is also a Japanese credit union, a senior citizens program aimed specifically at Japanese Americans, a Japanese American VFW post, and a Japanese Cultural Institute which filled the role of a community center for Japanese Americans. At the Institute various classes, meetings and social events took place.

So pervasive was the Japanese influence, that even the city sign welcoming people to Gardena was in the form of a Japanese gate. Many of the homes had quasi-Oriental architecture and landscaping. The public library had a Japanese garden and a well-known hamburger chain, while retaining its trademark arches, had chosen Oriental decor.

THE SETTING: ORANGE COUNTY

In Orange County, there were no concentrated areas of Japanese Americans as in Gardena and Los Angeles County in general. Rather, they were scattered throughout the various cities in the county. However, more are found in the more newly developed areas since the influx of young Japanese American families southward had been a recent trend.

Orange county had a tradition of being politically conservative and being WASPish in its population composition. It was difficult for

Asian Americans to purchase a home, particularly in the older and more affluent areas. The establishment of a few Asians in once totally white neighborhoods, as well as the housing boom, helped to open the door for many more new arrivals. These were generally young professionals of the second- and third-generations who were financially well-off.

Interestingly, in addition to this new community of second- and third-generation Japanese Americans, Orange county also had an older community of Japanese immigrants and their offspring. In the pre-war and early post-war years this area had many vegetable and fruit farms. Many of these old Japanese families were connected with agriculture, were in businesses serving the ethnic community, or were gardeners for the Orange county middle and upper classes. A number of them became quite wealthy, particularly with the skyrocketing value of their land (what were once family farms are now covered with houses or office buildings). In fact, one public school here was named after the Japanese farmer who donated the land for the school.

This community was not a geographic one. The various families were so widely scattered that usually there were at most a handful of Japanese American students in any one school. However, for many social activities and ceremonial events, such as weddings or funerals, the Japanese American families from all over Orange county were drawn together. The ethnic church, whether Christian or Buddhist, frequently served as focal point for this ethnic community; as with many other ethnic groups, it had far more than a religious function.

By the time of this research, the Japanese American ethnic community had grown far larger. New arrivals continued to move south into Orange county. With a larger population there appeared a few Oriental food stores, gift shops and restaurants, but these businesses were very few and widely scattered. They seem to be owned and operated by Japanese nationals rather than the *issei* or their offspring. On the surface it appears that the Japanese American population had totally assimilated into the mainly white suburbs of Orange county.

DIFFERENCES BETWEEN HIGH ETHNICS AND LOW ETHNICS

Both scholars and laymen have tended to view ethnicity as an ascriptive status - one is born into it. Consequently, any American of Japanese ancestry could be called an ethnic and a number of Japanese Americans could be interviewed to come up with "the" Japanese American identity.

In recent years, however, there has been some interest in delineating types of ethnic identity. Corrado (1975a, 1975b), for example, found in his work among the Welsh that there were at least four types of Welsh ethnic identity. Differences among Japanese Americans have also long been a popular topic of study, although the variations there were usually seen as characterizing the different generations, rather than varieties of ethnic identity (e.g., Feagin and Fujitaki 1972; Kitano 1961; Masuda, Matsumoto and Meredith 1970). The tendency has been to view the differences between generations as a case of each successive generation becoming increasingly Americanized.

In a study of third-generation Japanese American college students, Maykovitch (1972, 1973) did delineate a number of different types of *sansei* identity, based on attitudes and behavior as revealed through interviews. They are: a) the conformist *sansei* who accept the traditional values of diligence, conformity, and assimilation of their second-generation (*nisei*) parents, have a high achievement orientation and do well in school but are otherwise inconspicuous, due to their control of expression on the political, social or personal level; b) the liberated *sansei* who, while accepting the traditional values of diligence, conformity and assimilation, also show far more concern with social problems than do the conformist *sansei* and are actively involved in programs directed towards social improvement; c) the anomic *sansei* who reject the traditional values of their parents but are not involved in any sort of social issues; and d) the militant *sansei* who both reject the traditional values of the *nisei* and are actively involved in social issues, whether it means working for improvement within the existing social system in order to bring about social change (radical *sansei*) or working to destroy the existing social system in order to bring about social change (revolutionary *sansei*). Maykovitch feels that in general the *sansei* are characterized by their heterogeneity in comparison with the relatively homogeneous character of the first- and second-generations, although the majority of them appear to be of the conformist type.

Like the studies of Maykovitch and Corrado, my research focused on variations. I was not concerned, however, with identifying specific ethnic types, but rather with the range of <u>intensity of ethnicity</u> from low to high. While it was theoretically possible to find *sansei* of all four of Maykovich's types ranging throughout the ethnic scale this was not the purpose of the study. In fact, *sansei* of differing political persuasions (from people who were apolitical to those who had once belonged to the Yellow Power movement in the early 1970s) were found on the high ethnic end of the scale. In contrast to the many studies which have focused on *sansei* college students, this study concentrated mainly on older *sansei* who had completed their education (the average age was about 30 years) and efforts were made to conduct interviews in settings familiar to them (most were in the informants' homes, a few were in their work-places).

In order to maximize the contrast and obtain a clearer picture of why ethnicity persists, Phase 3 of the study was designed to obtain data for the comparison of the attitudes and behavior of those who were on the extreme ends of the scale, i.e., those who were most ethnic and those who were least ethnic vis-a-vis the rest of the sample. Many of the questions asked of these informants were taken from the original close-ended questionnaire and made into open-ended questions in which people were asked why they felt the way they did, how and why they had gotten involved in specific organizations and activities, etc. The questions were selected on the basis of how well they distinguished between high and low ethnics on the larger sample and fell under the categories that were used to construct the ethnic scale (Passing on the Heritage to One's Children, Psychological Identity, Perception of Differences and Activities and Behavior).

HOW HIGH AND LOW ETHNICS DID NOT DIFFER

Prior to exploring the differences that emerged in this study between high ethnics and low ethnics, it is of interest to briefly discuss what was found not to distinguish between the two groups. A number of researchers (e.g. Levine and Montero 1973) have thought that as an individual became more successful in the larger society, he would become more assimilated into the mainstream culture and less involved in the ethnic community. Education[1], occupation[2], and income[3] have frequently been used as partial measures of an individual's success; in this study no significant difference between the high ethnics and the low ethnics was found on any of these three variables, although there was a weak trend that lower ethnics had higher income levels. It would appear that socioeconomic success does not inevitably lead to the disappearance of ethnicity.

Levine and Montero (1973) in their study of the socioeconomic mobility among three generations of Japanese Americans feel there may be evidence for a growing schism within the Japanese American community. There is a well-educated, successful group who tend towards assimilation into the mainstream culture while avoiding heavy participation in the ethnic subculture, and a less educated, less prosperous group who remain in the ethnic community. One reason those of a lower socioeconomic level remain in the community may be due to their inability to cope successfully in the larger, general society. Meanwhile the training and skills that are necessary for success in American society and are valued by the *sansei* may so disperse the more assimilated segment of the generation geographically that a viable subculture can no longer be maintained. They state that there is little evidence for the rapid disappearance of the Japanese American subculture but it will apparently be a subculture maintained by those socioeconomically less successful. It may well be true as Levine and Montero state that those less well-off tend to gravitate more to the security of the geographically defined ethnic community. However, as will be discussed in the section on ethnicity in the suburbs, there may also be emerging a second type of ethnic community for the geographically scattered, upper middle-class ethnics.

SIGNIFICANT DIFFERENCES BETWEEN HIGH AND LOW ETHNICS[4]

Psychological Identification

The psychological identification of an individual with others of the same cultural origin, in a culturally plural society, is of crucial importance. According to De Vos:

> Ethnicity . . . is in its narrowest sense a feeling of continuity with the past, a feeling that is maintained as an essential part of one's self-definition. Ethnicity is also intimately related to the individual need for collective continuity. The individual senses to some degree a threat to his own survival if his group or lineage is threatened with

> extinction. Ethnicity, therefore, includes a sense of personal survival in the historical continuity of the group . . . Ethnicity in its deepest psychological level is a sense of survival. If one's group survives, one is assured of survival, even if not in a personal sense. (1975:17)

The data, as anticipated, reveals that the high ethnics tend to place relatively more importance on their identity as Japanese Americans than as Americans, feel more directly affected by what happens to other Japanese Americans and see the fact of their being Japanese American as playing a more important part in their lives than do the low ethnics. (Table 1, Appendix A summarizes the significant differences).

Japanese American Identity - A Sense of Survival

Informants were given four categories - American, Japanese American, Japanese and Asian American - and were asked to rank order them in terms of how they identified themselves. In the entire sample of 102, 66.3% identify first as Japanese American, 16.8% as American first, 11.8% as Asian American and 5.9% feel they are Japanese first. On the ethnic scale, when the top and bottom 25% of the sample are compared, a significant difference[5] emerges, with high ethnics identifying themselves as Japanese Americans before Americans while low ethnics tend to identify themselves first as American and only secondly as Japanese Americans. When asked to place themselves on a scale with "Americanness" on one end and "Japanese Americanness/Japaneseness" on the other the two groups differ with the high ethnics toward the Japanese Americanness/Japaneseness end of the scale. The two groups also differ in how important it is to them that a Japanese American identity continue to exist, and how upset they would be if Japanese Americans intermarried to such an extent that eventually there would no longer be any "pure" Japanese Americans in existence; as would be expected, high ethnics feel it is much more important to them that a Japanese American identity and a racially identifiable population continue to exist.

De Vos has stated that in its deepest sense ethnicity is a desire for survival of oneself indirectly through the continuation of the subculture that one strongly identifies with. Certainly this was a major theme that emerged during interviews with informants on this topic. In recent years the outmarriage rates of Japanese Americans have seemed to rise dramatically. Tinker (1973) and Kikumura and Kitano (1973) have found in surveys of marriage licenses issued over a period of years in Los Angeles, San Francisco, Fresno and Hawaii that the rate of outmarriage has approached, or even exceeded 50% for both males and females. Kikumura and Kitano hypothesize that this rate of outmarriage will continue to grow until there may eventually no longer be a racially "pure" Japanese American group.

The high ethnics in particular are aware of and express concern over this trend. Many have said they do not like it and hope their children won't do it, but seem to feel it is a trend that will be impossible to stop. With this racial assimilation they fear will come a loss of their ethnic cultural ties; to the high ethnics, being Japanese American is both a cultural and a racial identity. There are children of mixed marriages who identify mainly with the Japanese American side of themselves and interact heavily with other Japanese Americans. While they are accepted by the ethnic community (among their peers they are often seen as physically more attractive) it is still not the same for high ethnics. As one informant said, "I am a Japanese American and I would like to perpetuate what I am . . . [If there are no more pure Japanese Americans] the group I identify with would be gone." For these people part of ethnicity is a question of survival. Some high ethnics also fear the loss of a physically recognizable ethnic group because they feel that by blending into the larger American society what the Japanese

Americans did as a people will be forgotten. They feel they must remain visible as a minority and as united as possible if they, as Japanese Americans, hope to improve their position as a minority.

The low ethnics display less concern about the increasing rates of outmarriage among the *sansei*. While some feel it would be nice for a Japanese American ethnic group to remain in existence it is not crucial to their own lives. Furthermore, many separate race from culture and feel that as long as the Japanese American culture and heritage remains (although not necessarily that they themselves are part of it or are responsible for helping to perpetuate it) it does not matter if the race remains pure. Others also feel that assimilation is good because it is important to know other types of people and that remaining solely within one's ethnic community can often foster stereotypes and prejudice, both within and outside of the group.

One's Fate and Other Japanese Americans

In order to test if an individual who identifies strongly as a Japanese American would also identify strongly with other Japanese Americans and would feel that what happens to other Japanese Americans (or even Japanese) can potentially have an effect on his own life, informants were asked to rate how much they felt their own fate was bound up with the fate of other Americans. The high ethnics see their fate as much more bound to the fate of other Japanese Americans than do low ethnics. There is no significant difference between the answers of the two groups with regard to themselves and other Americans. For each individual it was then determined whether they felt their fate was more bound up with the fate of other Japanese Americans, other Americans, or equally bound up with both. To a greater extent high ethnics feel their fate is more bound up with other Japanese Americans than with other Americans than do the low ethnics. This identification was also tested by asking if they personally would feel insulted if a major newspaper were to insult Japanese Americans in general and if they would feel pleased if a major newspaper were to praise Japanese Americans. The two groups again differ significantly in that high ethnics believe they would both feel insulted and would feel pleased while low ethnics do not. Finally, it was felt that if an individual identifies strongly as a Japanese American he will more likely feel close to people of Japanese ancestry. Again this was borne out with significantly more high ethnics indicating that they feel closer to people of Japanese ancestry than to people of any other background.

Low ethnics, in general, tend to see themselves as individuals who basically succeed or fail in American society on their own merits and by their own efforts. High ethnics view themselves more as members of a group - a group which at times in its history has undergone extreme discrimination at the hands of the majority society and which they feel could still occur today. Because they physically look like Japanese nationals, many of them feel that even the actions of Japan can affect them; at times they become convenient, albeit inappropriate, targets for the larger community to vent its anger against Japan. For example, the Los Angeles Times in a Save Our Whales campaign urged its readers to boycott Japanese and Russian goods. As a result, Japanese Americans were by implication also targeted in this boycott. It is interesting to note that when asked whether they agree or disagree with the statement "One must act so as not to bring dishonor to the Japanese American community," there is a strong relationship between the respondent's answer and the degree of his ethnicity. The high ethnics tend to agree with the statement while the low ethnics do not.

Japanese American Influence on One's Life

Informants were asked to rate on a four-point scale how important a part in their lives is the fact that they are Japanese American. Low ethnics tend to see the fact of their being Japanese American as having little or no importance in their lives; high ethnics feel it is more important.

Perception of Differences between Japanese Americans and the Outside Society

Ethnic identity, behavior, and activities place an individual in one group or another. In essence, boundaries are drawn which include some people who are then deemed "insiders", or "in-group members", and exclude others - the "outsiders". The premise on which lines are drawn is that those on one side are different from those on the other side (Barth 1969).

In comparing the high ethnics with the low ethnics significant differences emerge. High ethnics feel they differ far more from the American norm on a number of dimensions than do the low ethnics. Low ethnics feel their ways of life are nearly identical to the rest of the society.

This does not mean that high ethnics are less acculturated or more Japanese, for often times the high ethnics see themselves as very different from the Japanese nationals. It is interesting to note that there is some antagonism between the Japanese Americans and the Japanese nationals with whom they have contact. Frequently Japanese businessmen and their families are sent to work in an American branch of their parent company for a limited period before returning to Japan. Common complaints about those who live in Gardena are that they are rude, overly aggressive, noisy, dirty and poor disciplinarians of their children. High ethnics tend to see themselves as more Japanese American in their ways, a subculture which is different from both American and Japanese culture.

When questioned about the ways in which they feel they differ as Japanese Americans from American culture, high ethnics find it easy to delineate the differences while low ethnics find it far more difficult. On some dimensions both high and low ethnics might follow a custom (e.g., gift-giving practices) which differs from the American pattern, but low ethnics either are unaware that their practice is different, or if they are aware do not view the differences as important. High ethnics are aware of the difference and feel that they are significant markers which set them off from the rest of American society. If low ethnics do see some of their practices as different, they usually view the differences as Japanese and tend to focus on the material objects involved (e.g., they like Japanese music or have Japanese art objects in their homes). High ethnics see the differences as more Japanese American and focus on behavioral and value differences.

Outlook on Life and Values and Beliefs

Informants were asked to rate themselves on a four-point scale in terms of how much they felt they were like the rest of American society (the scale ran from "American" on one end to "Japanese American/Japanese" on the other). High ethnics see themselves as significantly more Japanese American in their outlook on life, and in their values and beliefs. In other words, high ethnics see themselves as differing more in these areas from the American "norm" while the low ethnics see little or no difference between themselves and other people. Not only are high ethnics more aware of differences between themselves and the rest of American society, but they often appear to be far more bothered by the lack of certain values and behavior in the larger society. By playing by different rules (which operate well when among other Japanese Americans) these Japanese Americans feel themselves to be at a disadvantage when operating in the outside community. They would not discard these values or behaviors, however, because they felt them to be superior.

The differences most often cited by high ethnics, and perhaps which put them most in a disadvantageous position in interacting with nonJapanese Americans, are the strong values placed on reciprocity, generosity, and hospitality. Japanese Americans, especially the high ethnics, are a very gift-giving people. When visiting a friend's home (particularly when invited for a meal), when a friend is very ill, is going on a trip, is celebrating a birthday, or had done one a favor, they bring a gift. There is a strong feeling of obligation about this. Women, in particular, have mentioned agonizing over what type of gift is proper and how much they should spend.

The gift-giving does not end there. Sometime in the future, on an appropriate occasion, the recipient must reciprocate. In this way the relationship is (ideally) never terminated. A number of informants mentioned that before they leave for a major trip abroad, relatives and close friends often give them gifts of money which might be quite sizable - up to $50 or more. On the surface, this is to be considered "pocket money" for the individual while on his trip. In actuality, the traveller is now under obligation to bring back a gift or *omiyage* from his trip for each giver. The value of the return gift has to relate to the amount of money given -i.e., a larger amount of money requires a larger or better souvenir. At some time in the future, in addition to the *omiyage*, the traveller is also obligated to give the original giver (or some member of his family) a gift of money when he goes on a trip and this person, in turn, now is obligated to bring back *omiyage* and so on.

High ethnics have often said they are aggravated by what they perceive to be the stinginess of white people. Following the rules of conduct thought to be correct, Japanese Americans will fight to be the one to pay the dinner check and will be the first to offer to help out. This system functions well when it involves other Japanese Americans since they all know and adhere to the same rules, but it breaks down when nonJapanese Americans are included. Japanese Americans complain that nonJapanese Americans allow them to continually pick up the check and are slow to reciprocate. As a result, these Japanese Americans feel they are taken advantage of.

The choices in interacting with nonJapanese Americans are to continue to be taken advantage of, to stop adhering to the rule of reciprocity and become like other Americans, or to limit one's interactions with nonJapanese Americans. Some high ethnics have found a fourth solution - they follow two rules of conduct which they selectively apply depending upon whom they are interacting with. In a relationship where both parties are Japanese American they are far more aware of and conscientious about reciprocity and take more care and are more generous in the selection of gifts and hospitality. In a relationship in which one of the parties is nonJapanese American, they are more casual (and are aware that they are) - they will still reciprocate but will not go to as much trouble as they would if it involved Japanese Americans. For example, if a Japanese American child attends a birthday party for a caucasian friend the mother may buy a gift that is under $5 while if the child attends a birthday party for a Japanese American friend a more expensive gift will be purchased. Likewise, they expect far less from a caucasian than from a Japanese American.

Low ethnics, on the other hand, if aware of the difference, generally don't appear disturbed by it. Frequently they stated that, given a choice, they prefer the more casual attitudes of the American culture and see the elaborate gift-giving system of the ethnic Japanese Americans as somewhat burdensome. They favor a greater spontaneity in their generosity (for example, sharing some extra vegetables from their garden) and dislike the feeling of obligation to reciprocate that underlies much of the Japanese American system of gift-giving.

Another value often cited by high ethnics as differing between Japanese Americans and nonJapanese Americans is the emphasis placed on the closeness of the family. They feel that Japanese American parents do more for their children and spend much more on them. It is generally their experience that for school fund-raising functions or youth organization activities it is the Japanese American parents who turn out most regularly to help, who take the time to bake refreshments rather than buy them at a store, and who can be counted on to support any activities that are geared to helping the youth of the community A feeling commonly expressed belief in the community is that if a cause is for the benefit of the children or the elderly the Japanese Americans are very quick to support it. Japanese Americans also feel that they do not encourage their children to disengage from parental control as quickly as or to the extent that their nonJapanese American peers seem to do. Consequently, even when they reach adulthood children are not as independent from their families as they perceive nonJapanese Americans to be. They continue to consult their parents in many of their decisions and place a good deal of weight on the parents' opinions. Even if they live apart from their parents many *sansei* live nearby and go home to visit at least once a week, whereas their caucasian friends seem to visit their families far less.

As they are now in the process of raising their own families, the adult *sansei* are becoming more aware and appreciative of how much their parents have done for them and given to them. With the second-generation aging and reaching retirement there is, at least in the abstract, the desire as well as the feeling of obligation on the part of their *sansei* children to take care of them in their old age. Some are willing to have their parents live with them if necessary although others are against it, feeling it is too difficult to have two women in one kitchen. However, many are also opposed to the idea of placing the aging parents in an old person's home unless the parents desire to go there.

The families of low ethnics may or may not differ in their closeness from those of high ethnics, but low ethnics do not see, or at least cite, it as a Japanese American difference. In fact, a major difference between high and low ethnics with regard to "ethnic" behavior is that high ethnics have no trouble pointing out the differences in life style between themselves and nonJapanese Americans, while low ethnics often are unable to think of any differences. This is not to say that low ethnics do not at times hold to similar values as the high ethnics. Although there is a significant relationship between one's level of ethnicity and whether or not one feels obligated to reciprocate all favors and kindnesses, the relationship is modest - many low ethnics still feel it is good to reciprocate, but balked at the feeling of being obligated to do so. In many areas low and high ethnics are very similar in behavior, but a discrepancy lies in the fact that high ethnics are very aware of the differences between Japanese Americans and others, believe that these differences are of importance to them, and are used to drawing a boundary between themselves and nonJapanese Americans.

Way of Relating to People

Informants were asked to rank themselves on a series of scales in terms of whether they felt their ways of relating to people, dealing with them, and interacting with them were more Japanese

American or more American (generalized). In comparing their responses a significant difference again emerges between high and low ethnics - high ethnics see themselves as more Japanese American, as different from the rest of American society in their ways of relating to people whereas the low ethnics see less, if any, distinction between themselves and other Americans.

This may be the area of deepest division between high ethnic Japanese Americans and other Americans, and yet is one of the most difficult areas to study. Most high ethnic Japanese Americans questioned agree that there are unwritten rules of behavior in the Japanese American community and that these rules differ from those of the outside society. But what these rules are, specifically, is very difficult for most of them to articulate. It is acknowledged that Japanese Americans behave differently from nonJapanese Americans, and these differences play an important role in whether a person feels comfortable or uncomfortable in interacting with nonJapanese Americans. Again there is a split between the high ethnics and the low ethnics on this question. High ethnics tend to feel more comfortable with other Japanese Americans while low ethnics tend to feel more comfortable with nonJapanese Americans.

Whether the Japanese American patterns of behavior and rules of conduct in interpersonal relations are holdovers or survivals from a Japanese way of life is a question left unexplored in research. It has been suggested that some of the Japanese American ways of relating to people are not of Japanese origin so much as a response and a survival strategy of a powerless minority group to majority group domination. Such practices as being passive and keeping from freely expressing one's emotions are viewed as forming a useful strategy for first-generation immigrants when dealing with the established white power structure. This behavior pattern, being a successful strategy, was then socialized into the offspring of the immigrants and became the accepted norm. It was given legitimacy by considering it as a cultural heritage rather than a response to the lack of power. Whatever the origin of the differences, the important point is that the differences do exist, at least for the high ethnics. These differences form an important basis upon which third-generation Japanese Americans set themselves apart from the rest of American society, even though according to many objective standards they are totally acculturated to American society. English is their native language and very few speak Japanese. They wear western clothing, few owning or knowing how to properly wear a *kimono*. They eat rice but also potatoes, bread and *tortillas*. They join the boy and girl scouts and the Optimists clubs, and the majority go to Christian churches. If they go to Japan they feel just as much like foreigners and tourists as they would if they went to Italy.

Yet there are differences, far more subtle and complex, and presumably more deeply rooted than the easily identifiable traditional differences of language, dress, cuisine, religion and folk customs. Ways of relating to people are largely learned unconsciously during the socialization process, something one grows up with, and a person is less likely to be aware of differences in the ways he and others relate than in more obvious differences such as the use of chopsticks instead of a fork. It is also much more difficult to change the way one relates to others than to change the particular utensil one uses for eating. A person interacts with others in the way that he assumes to be natural and human. If some seem not to respond in the "proper" manner while others do, he may assume that something is wrong with those who are different, even if he cannot explain to himself why they are wrong. However, he knows, or senses that he does not feel comfortable with them and avoids interacting with them whenever possible. For high ethnic third-generation Japanese Americans, much more than simply symbolic differences remain.

The differences that high ethnics perceive as existing between Japanese Americans and nonJapanese Americans are briefly covered here and expanded upon in the section on ethnic style and Japanese American culture.

Often cited differences between the way Japanese Americans interact with other people and the way nonJapanese Americans do (particularly caucasians, the group the Japanese Americans most often compare themselves to) are that Japanese Americans are more polite, less aggressive, more formal in manner, less likely to disclose personal information and less individualistic in orientation (Arkoff 1959; Connor 1976; Schwartz 1971). Many of these interaction patterns are learned and reinforced mainly when one has regular or heavy contact with other Japanese Americans. A Japanese American who has been raised among primarily nonJapanese American peers has had his interaction patterns modified into ones more nearly approaching those of the American norm. As a result, such an individual feels uneasy with other Japanese Americans who act differently from what he has become accustomed to. High ethnics view this individual as a "banana" - yellow on the outside but white on the inside - and tend to avoid him unless he conforms to the norms that they are familiar with.

Aggression, directness and individualism seem to be among the traits that are valued in the larger society, particularly for men. Among the *sansei*, however, people displaying these traits are labelled as pushy, hostile and rude. High ethnics, in particular, are raised with the idea that one should be aware of other people and take care not to hurt their feelings. Consequently they are uncomfortable in any sort of confrontation situation and try in all ways to avoid conflict. Rather than directly dealing with it, *sansei* prefer to let a problem "slide". If, for example, a Japanese American is upset with a person's behavior he does not directly inform the offending party, because that is rude and likely to hurt the person's feelings. Rather, by indirect, nonconfronting methods, such as speaking less with and behaving more formally toward the individual, or by canceling a social engagement previously made with the person, the target individual gradually begins to realize that the relationship is not the way it used to be and should be, and that he has done something wrong. He becomes aware of disapproval even though at no time is he ever directly told that he has caused displeasure, much less what it is he has done wrong. Nor is it proper for him to confront the offended individual and ask 1) is he upset? or 2) why is he upset? It is not unheard of for an individual to know that he has offended, but not how he has offended. In order for the relationship to continue, the offender must make a circumspect apology while the person who has been offended denies that anything was wrong in the first place. At other times the relationship is temporarily suspended and then resumed once the offended person is no longer upset. At no time is anyone confronted, nor is there a direct acknowledgement by the parties involved that a problem exists. Anyone who was not trained under these rules of conduct and therefore attempts to rectify problems by more direct means is seen as causing the other party embarrassment and to lose face. He will alienate the individual he hoped to placate and probably will fail to solve the problem.

The rugged individualist is not normally a type that is admired among the high ethnic Japanese Americans. Often times informants expressed the feeling that one reason they are uncomfortable with nonJapanese Americans is that they feel "different" when they are the only Asian in a group of occidentals. Conformity, particularly within one's close social network, is important. It is conformity both in appearance and behavior, and it can be judged down to such details as the particular brand of shoes one wears or the store one shops at. Parents want their children to have the same things as their playmates because they don't want their children to be different from the others.

In contrast to many nonJapanese Americans, high ethnic Japanese Americans tend to be less tolerant of differences and group control of their members is tight. In dealing with a straying member there is no overt action as one might expect. Social control is maintained by ridicule and ostracism. Rather than the members of a group directly informing an errant member that he has strayed too far from the group's norms they will, instead, ridicule him in front of the group, thereby hopefully shaming him into conformity. To the uninitiated outsider, harmonious relationships appear uninterrupted while in actuality, beneath the surface, group control is being exercised. Even within more formal group situations, such as clubs and service organizations, there is less likely to be found strong individualistic officers making decisions for the group. Japanese American groups, even among the *sansei*, tend to operate by formal consensus - individuals don't like to be openly disruptive and tend to follow group decisions, even if they are not totally in agreement with them. Consequently, coming to a decision can be a long, drawn-out process. But high ethnics feel it is worth the trouble since in this way no individual or group faction is offended or alienated.

Way of Raising Children

Informants were asked whether they felt their methods of child socialization were in some way distinctive of Japanese Americans and thereby different from the American pattern in general. Again the two groups varied, with high ethnics differentiating themselves in this area while low ethnics group themselves with the outside society.

As in other areas a major difference between high and low ethnics is that high ethnics find it far easier to delineate what a Japanese American method of child socialization is, both as it applies to themselves and as it applies in general to Japanese Americans as a group. Low ethnics, on the other hand, usually see little if any differences between their child raising methods and those of the rest of American society. They are also unable to generalize as to what the more "traditional" Japanese Americans do. Other low ethnics feel their methods are somewhat Japanese American in that they try to stress the closeness of the family and respect for elders. This is a base to which they deliberately try to add what they feel are more American ways, such as greater freedom in terms of physical contact and expression of affection, less unquestioning acceptance of authority, more self-reliance and independence on the part of the child, and a better ability to express oneself verbally. It is acknowledged that should they succeed in inculcating these traits in their children, these children are less likely to fit into the ethnic community. However, fitting into the Japanese American community is not of high priority for these low ethnic parents.

High ethnics feel that they as Japanese Americans are much stricter with and more demanding of their children. They feel they are more concerned with their children's good behavior and good performances in school than are many of their caucasian counterparts. They have noticed that they tend to put more restrictions on their children's activities for a longer period of time and keep them closer to home or under some sort of familial supervision until a later age than is often the norm among their children's nonJapanese American friends. Some mothers, in fact, prefer their children to play at the homes of Japanese Americans rather than nonJapanese Americans because they feel more certain that at a Japanese American's home they will be closely supervised thereby assuring their safety; at a nonJapanese American's home the children will be allowed too much unsupervised freedom which could lead to an accident.

It is also of interest to note that this strong parental supervision on the part of Japanese American families, or at least high ethnic Japanese American families, is not seen by these people as a Japanese trait. Particularly for the Gardena Japanese Americans, who come in contact with the Japanese business company families, they feel that these children from Japan are spoiled brats who are allowed to run wild and get into mischief without being punished for it. They see these children misbehave in public - running and shouting through the halls or climbing on and jumping off furniture - without any sign of disapproval from their mothers. The Japanese American mothers compare these children to their own who would not be allowed to act in this fashion and would be disciplined if they did.

This close supervision which continues for a more prolonged period results in the slower social development of Japanese American children, particularly the boys. Compared to their caucasian age-mates the boys seem less assured in the social graces and begin dating at a later age. This was one of the complaints of *sansei* females about *sansei* males - while caucasian males are already somewhat sophisticated in male-female relationships, the Japanese American male still prefers to remain with his male buddies and is very shy and uneasy about approaching females. At the age that many American youths are dating, many Japanese Americans continue to socialize in single-sex or mixed groups.

High ethnic informants also mentioned that they demand more of their children in every way. Some have said that while they tell their children that all that is expected of them is to do the best they can, their own unstated view is that their children had better bring home A's on their report cards or come in first in a contest.

However, just as they expect more from their children (better behavior, more respect for their elders, better grades), mothers also feel they do much more for their children than do caucasian mothers. Some place the relationship with their children above the relationship with their husbands, even though they realize that eventually the children will grow up and leave the home, leaving the mother alone with her husband. High ethnic mothers believe that Japanese American women center their lives more around the children and families while nonJapanese American women allocate more time to spend on their own interests or with their husbands.

Case Study:

Shortly after spending several hours one afternoon questioning Carol, a *sansei* housewife, I had an opportunity to observe the difference in attitudes expressed by a few Japanese American mothers and a caucasian friend in regards to their children. These differing attitudes seem to illustrate some of the points brought out on child socialization I had discussed with both low and high ethnics.

Ruth, Carol's caucasian roommate in college, and her husband and son had just moved to Orange county from the East. She had stopped in to visit. Also present were two of Carol's friends, both Japanese American. All of the women were upper middle-class suburban wives of professional men. Over coffee in the kitchen the women chatted about a number of topics, among which was the subject of present day education. Ruth, the caucasian friend, felt that children are put under too much stress now. She complained that her son would get upset every day that she forgot to buy the tissue paper he needed for an Easter project in school (the teacher gave them a month's notice). If a child forgot to bring in the tissue paper by the day of the project he couldn't make anything, since obviously he didn't have the necessary materials. The caucasian mother felt this was wrong since she felt the schools weren't teaching the students responsibility by requiring them to bring in their own paper by a certain date, but were only teaching the mothers. In addition, she felt the children having to supply their own tissue for a project was illegal, since she believed that the state was supposed to supply all materials in public schools. She also objected to the fact that her son already had homework and is only in the first grade. As proof that children today have too much pressure put on them by the educational system she went on to relate that her son is having some problems with his vision and is on the borderline of needing glasses. She asked the doctor if his problems could be caused by stress; he agreed that it was a possibility.

While Ruth was complaining the three Japanese American women listened. None of them directly disagreed with her but neither did any of them appear to agree with what she was saying. Instead, they related stories of how they dealt with their own children. Carol, whose husband is a second-generation Japanese American, mentioned that she felt her husband's generation was able to get through school successfully even though their parents usually did not speak English. Because of their lack of facility with English the *issei* couldn't help their children since they often did not know what was happening in school. She felt that perhaps why her fourth-generation children have difficulties in learning responsibility is because she reminds them so they can't forget - when they are ready to leave for school she asks each of them at the door if they all have their lunches and homework. Diane, a Japanese American mother, recalled that once her son telephoned her from school to ask her to bring his saxophone, which he had forgotten at home, so he could take his music lesson. She did it because it was the first time it had happened but as she handed him his instrument she told him, "Don't let it happen again." He happened to forget it again one day but the bus had not yet arrived so he was able to race home and back just in time to catch the bus. Diane concluded by saying that she hoped someday when her children forget something very important that she will have the strength to refuse to bring it to them. The two Japanese Americans agreed with her.

When Ruth, the caucasian, objected to her son having homework in the first grade, since she felt it put too much stress on a child at too early an age, Diane simply commented that her children had homework when they were in the first grade. Ruth also was against homework in elementary school because she felt that at that age it is the parents who end up doing it. The Japanese American women agreed that that can happen but then went on to state that they help their children if they need it but they try to be careful not to actually do the work for their children.

Feeling Different

Informants were given a list of occasions and situations and asked on which of those, if any, they felt more Japanese/Japanese American or were more aware of being Japanese American. A significantly greater number of high ethnics feel more Japanese or Japanese American, or were aware of their Japaneseness or Japanese Americanness, in more situations than are low ethnics.

As for the specific occasions, there are no significant differences between high and low ethnics in terms of awareness of being Japanese American on religious occasions, at political events, in one's occupation, during family occasions or when with other Japanese Americans. On family occasions, and when with other Japanese Americans, over half of both high and low ethnics indicate they are at times more aware of being Japanese American; less than 40% of each group indicated such an awareness at religious and political events. Significant differences between high and low ethnics in awareness of being Japanese American emerge in the following:

when with nonJapanese Americans, at Japanese cultural events, at social or recreational events, at organizational meetings, and when in unfamiliar cities or situations. The results are summarized in Table 2, Appendix A.

Individual informants' answers for why they feel more Japanese American on certain occasions covered a wide range of reasons, but certain common themes emerged. Basically, high ethnics dislike being different, being a minority and standing out in a group, which they feel is the case when their physical appearance sets them apart from Americans of nonAsian ancestry. "When I go to a different city where there are few Japanese I feel more Japanese and therefore, different . . . it's uncomfortable to feel different." They prefer being in groups they can blend physically into. They find it easier to get along and communicate with other Japanese Americans who have similar viewpoints and behaviors. Low ethnics seem to encounter fewer occasions when they are aware of being Japanese American because they often do not mind looking different or being the only Asian in a group. Consequently, they do not necessarily feel different from the others when in a nonJapanese American group. In fact, for some it is only when they are with a large group of Japanese Americans in public that they become aware they are part of a group which is different in the larger society. (See Appendix A, Table 3 for summary statistics on Perception of Differences).

Activities and Behavior

Psychological identification with a group is an important aspect of ethnic identity, as is an awareness that differences exist between this ethnic group and others, and the larger society. However, psychological identification is not in itself adequate, although De Vos feels that "[e]thnicity is determined by what a person feels about himself, not by how he is observed to behave" (1975:17). An individual must also signal his group identity to outsiders and, more importantly, to members of his own group. This is done by his actions and behavior as well as the activities he takes part in. If ethnicity were determined only by what a person feels about himself, it would be possible for an individual to identify primarily as a Japanese American and yet, by his actions be totally rejected by other Japanese Americans; similarly, it would be possible for an individual to reject associating with other Japanese Americans although he psychologically identifies as a Japanese American. Just such a person was encountered in the course of this research. He feels he is very ethnic, sees himself as very Japanese American in his values and beliefs, outlook and orientation, and yet associates with other Japanese Americans only rarely and does not feel the need or desire to do so. As for his children, he feels that he can teach them at home everything they need to know about being Japanese American and therefore it is not necessary for them to be with other Japanese Americans.

By its very nature ethnicity is a social phenomenon - it serves to exclude some people and to include others. It includes face-to-face contact and interaction among members of the same group. To move from <u>category</u> to a functioning <u>group</u> there needs to be some sort of common base to work from. Physical appearance is not enough - Japanese Americans who do not fall within the range of acceptable Japanese American behavior are not accepted by the ethnic community as "real" Japanese Americans. Some informants who were raised mainly in nonJapanese American areas and who have little knowledge of Japanese American behavior, in their search for identity feel a desire to get to know other Japanese Americans better. However, when they attempt to do so they often find themselves rebuffed unless they are willing to change their behavior to a more

Japanese American style or else they themselves dislike interacting with Japanese Americans when they discover how different at times it is.

Importance of Associating with Other Japanese Americans

To be ethnic the particular things one does are not as important as the fact that one does them with other ethnics. Be it pounding rice to make New Year's cakes, wearing a *kimono* and doing Japanese folk dances at the midsummer *obon* festival, attending a bible study group, taking part as a team member in a basketball tournament or putting on a swimsuit and parading down a runway in a beauty contest, what makes these activities ethnic is that they are done with other Japanese Americans. These activities increase and/or intensify interaction with fellow ethnics while at the same time excluding or limiting the participation of nonJapanese Americans. High ethnics are aware of this social nature of ethnicity and feel more than low ethnics, that it is important to associate with other Japanese Americans.

The emphasis placed on their being with other Japanese Americans is born out in their friendship and dating patterns. Not only do high ethnics have a greater proportion of their friendships with other Japanese Americans, but most or all of their closest friends are Japanese American. When asked whom they have dated, starting with their high school years, it was found that high ethnics tend to date mostly Japanese Americans while low ethnics generally date mostly nonJapanese Americans or a mixed group of Japanese Americans and nonJapanese Americans (about 50% each). Even in this area Japanese Americans, especially high ethnics, perceive differences in the dating behavior of Japanese Americans and caucasians. Caucasians appear to Japanese Americans to approach dating far more casually and are more skilled, more outgoing and more comfortable in their relations with the opposite sex. Both Japanese American males and females are seen as shyer, less aggressive, and less sophisticated in their dating behavior. Some informants have characterized the difference of a first date with a Japanese American and with a caucasian as sitting in painful silence with occasional periods of stilted conversation with the former and comfortable, easy-going conversation with the latter. Relationships with the opposite sex appear to be viewed with less casualness, at least among the more ethnic Japanese Americans, and consequently their dating pattern tends to be one of sequential rather than concurrent relationships. Rather than managing a number of casual relationships at the same time, they prefer to date steadily one individual for a longer period of time (often years) and terminate one relationship before beginning another. They might express some admiration for the ease with which caucasians seem to handle a number of relationships but many of them feel very uncomfortable if it occurs in their lives. Such was the case with a female informant in her early 20s who had begun to steadily date one male after reluctantly terminating a relationship with a previous boyfriend who then returned after a number of months. She had not dated either one long enough to seriously consider marriage but found she liked both of them. She started to date both but admitted she felt very uncomfortable doing this and wished the situation had never occurred.

Ethnic Patronage and Support

As well as preferring in their close personal relationships to be with other Japanese Americans, high ethnics also differ from low ethnics in their affiliations. They are more likely to help other Japanese Americans and to belong to a Japanese American service, community or social organization.

Significantly more high ethnics are likely to make a contribution when the person asking for the contribution is Japanese American, regardless of whether or not the cause is sponsored by Japanese Americans or is specifically aimed at helping Japanese Americans. In addition, of the estimated total yearly amount each family gives for charity in terms of money, time, services and material donations, high ethnics estimate that they give a higher proportion to specifically Japanese American causes than low ethnics. (Low ethnics tend to donate mainly to organizations that serve the general nonethnic community). There are two major reasons given for the support of Japanese American charities. First, by contributing to a Japanese American cause it is helping one's "own kind" and, in this way, helping oneself. Second, it is assumed that Japanese Americans are more honest and Japanese American organizations more trustworthy. Therefore, any money given is for a worthwhile cause and correctly used, whereas they are not always so trusting of nonJapanese American organizations. As a result, they give readily and unquestioningly when asked to help support a Japanese American cause, but view nonJapanese American charities a little more warily.

In addition to these admitted reasons for supporting Japanese American charities, it can also be postulated that guilt, obligation and a desire to maintain status in the ethnic community play a role for the high ethnics. As a member of an ethnic community, high ethnics often know personally or know of quite a number of Japanese Americans in the area. They would feel obligated to help a friend's or acquaintance's organization and would feel guilty to refuse. Thus they contribute even when they really do not care to. Because communication networks are often very effective in an ethnic community and high ethnics care a great deal about the opinions of their fellow ethnics, they also feel more compelled to support Japanese American causes. This desire to maintain their standing in the ethnic community as well as the competitiveness of many Japanese Americans within an ethnic setting can at times be used to help increase support of a particular cause. For example, prospective contributors will be told in confidence the amount other people have contributed. This, of course, pressures them to contribute at least as much, if they do not wish to be outdone. In one organization that is successful in raising money, a donation booklet is printed with the contributors' names on white, silver or gold pages, depending on the amount donated. Even for events where one is not approached directly, this system can be used very effectively. In Los Angeles, during a cultural festival called *Nisei* Week, many supposedly free exhibitions of flower arrangements, tea ceremony, sword displays, calligraphy and the like are held. However, at the entrance to every exhibit, there is a large clear glass fish bowl in which dollar bills are conspicuously placed. A Japanese American attendant sits next to it so that no one can pass by without seeing the "voluntary donation" bowl and being noticed by the attendant.

High ethnics are more likely to vote for a political candidate if he or she is Japanese American than are low ethnics. The reasons for this action are more mixed - some feel a Japanese American politician will inherently be more honest and so is seen as a better person; some feel a Japanese American will be more aware of and therefore more responsive to Japanese American problems and needs; some feel that having a Japanese American as a politician will help improve the image of Japanese Americans in general as well as serving as a role model for their children. They do not necessarily feel he will be a better politician, since they feel that caucasians are more aggressive and therefore, if honest, more effective in politics. Others feel that, out of curiosity, they might be more likely to read the Japanese American candidate's positions on various issues and thus feel more informed about him when it is time to vote. Finally, many stated that all things being equal, the fact that an individual is Japanese American will tip their vote to his side.

High ethnics are also more willing to use their influence to help a person get a job if the individual in question is Japanese American. Where low ethnics tend to feel one must make a decision according to the qualifications of each individual, regardless of racial background, high ethnics are more willing to generalize. They feel from their own experiences that a Japanese American is usually a better, more diligent and more dependable worker so there is less likelihood of such a person disappointing and embarrassing them if they recommend him to their superiors or they themselves hire him. It is also acknowledged, however, that things may be changing; although none ever stated they have personally met one, some have heard tales of third-generation Japanese Americans who are lazy and unreliable employees.

Except for subscribing to or regularly reading a Japanese American newspaper, there is no significant difference between low and high ethnics in terms of their patronage of services offered by other Japanese Americans. Whether low or high ethnic, more than half of the smaller sample turn to a fellow Japanese American for certain services - of those who have doctors 51% go to a Japanese American doctor, 82% go to a Japanese American dentist, 71% go to a Japanese American optometrist, 63% go to a Japanese American insurance agent and 58% bank or save at one of the growing number of Japan-based banks in California. In the larger sample of 102 this same tendency holds as well. An important reason for this pattern is that generally Japanese Americans (and probably most others as well) do not select health service personnel randomly, but patronize them on the strength of a family member's or friend's recommendation. Since their family is Japanese American and some or many of their friends are Japanese American, it follows that there is a better chance of their being linked into a Japanese American network in terms of this aspect of their lives. Many informants stated that their second-generation parents or good friends of their parents recommended the physician they presently see.

Only 30% of the sample subscribe to an ethnic newspaper, but there is a significant difference between high and low ethnics: 88% of the low ethnics do not subscribe or read a Japanese American newspaper while almost half of the high ethnics do.

Ethnic Activities and Events

High ethnics also attend Japanese American events and participate in Japanese American activities far more often than do low ethnics. What makes the following occasions ethnic in nature and therefore, important for the maintenance of ethnicity, is not that they involve a display of Japanese culture. These events bring Japanese Americans in contact with each other as spectators and participants, workers and patrons, and serve to symbolize for the people their identity as Japanese Americans and as members of an ethnic group. High ethnics attend with greater frequency the *obon* festivals, midsummer carnivals and folk dances given by every Japanese American Buddhist church. They are ostensibly to honor the spirits of one's ancestors, but in actuality have come to be more of a Japanese American ethnic community occasion in which both Buddhists and Christians take part. High ethnics also attend *Nisei* Week activities more often than do low ethnics. *Nisei* Week was begun before World War II as a community festival for and by the maturing second-generation and was held in Little Tokyo, the Japanese section of metropolitan Los Angeles. At present it actually runs for nearly a month in the summer, climaxing the final week with an increased number of exhibits and activities including a parade, street dances and a carnival. Activities range from golf, tennis and swimming tournaments to fashion shows to "prettiest baby" contests to martial arts and Japanese cultural exhibits, to beauty contests and coronation balls. High ethnics also go to Japanese American carnivals more often, are more likely to attend ceremonial dinners given by Japanese American organizations, attend more Japanese American social dances, go more often to Japanese American sports events, either as spectators or competitors, attend more Japanese and Japanese American entertainment shows, go to more educational talks given by Japanese Americans or dealing with topics of concern to Japanese Americans, participate more frequently in picnics, beach parties, etc. that are attended exclusively, or nearly exclusively, by Japanese Americans and are more likely to go on trips and overnight excursions with other Japanese Americans.

Through these activities, many of which are not based on traditional Japanese culture, *sansei* who so desire can lead at least the noninstrumental portion of their lives in a nearly exclusively Japanese American environment. Here they can be the majority culture and do things in the way in which they feel most comfortable, with people who understand them and are doing things in the same way. (Summary statistics in Appendix A, Table 4).

Passing on the Heritage

Informants were asked six questions regarding their children and on all of them significant differences emerge between high and low ethnics. For high ethnics there is a greater desire on their part that their children - the fourth-generation - remain ethnic as well.

It is much more important to high ethnics that their children identify as Japanese Americans. They identify as Japanese Americans and they are concerned that the Japanese Americans may becoming an extinct "race" due to the high rates of intermarriage. They feel it is important that some sort of Japanese American identity continue to exist. In terms of social ethnic ties, the two groups were particularly divided. High ethnics are more likely to feel it is very important that their children have friendships with other Japanese Americans, date Japanese Americans and marry Japanese Americans, while low ethnics are far less concerned about the cultural origin of their children's friends, dates and spouses. High ethnics tend to stress the importance of being with people like themselves in order to minimize difficulties while low ethnics feel it is important to learn how to relate well to all types of people. High ethnics place somewhat more stress on group similarities, i.e., "Japanese Americans share the same values, traditions and behaviors which make for easier communication", while low ethnics appear to place more emphasis on the individual, i.e., "what's important in a friend are his individual qualities rather than his race".

High ethnics also want their children to have Japanese American friends because in this way they hope the chances of their dating and marrying Japanese Americans will be improved. This group places Japanese Americans in the "most preferred" potential mate category, followed by other Asian Americans who are very closely followed by caucasians. Mexican Americans and Black Americans are placed in the highly undesirable category as potential mates for their children. The two groups also differ significantly in that high ethnics feel it is more important for their children to maintain ties with the ethnic community. Ties through participation in various ethnic organizations are seen as important in helping their children to learn Japanese American culture as well as giving them opportunities to interact with and become friends with other Japanese Americans.

The final questions dealt with acquisition of culture. Although the majority of the informants (86%) in the smaller sample feel it is very important their children know something about their heritage, low ethnics are more likely to place less importance on this. In particular, a knowledge of Japanese American history, values, traditions and holiday celebrations are emphasized, for it is felt that by knowing of their heritage the children will take pride in being Japanese American. It is also interesting that even though most informants, whether high or low ethnics, do not know enough Japanese to speak it (beyond a few common expressions), high ethnics also think it is more important that their children learn Japanese than do low ethnics. Most do not know the language, have subsequently come to regret it and as a result want their children to learn it.

Even though high ethnics very much desire that their children also remain ethnic, most of them feel that ultimately their children's happiness comes first. Therefore, they do not intend to openly forbid interactions with white peers. Rather, they hope that by encouraging their children to participate in ethnic organizations and events, by socializing as a family with other Japanese American families and by continually showing them the Japanese American alternatives, e.g. "Why don't you try dating a Japanese American girl? They're nice too," they can subtly make their desires clear to their offspring and gently steer them into a more Japanese American world. (See Appendix A, Table 5 for summary of statistics).

Miscellaneous Questions

Although not included in the ethnic score analysis, several other differences also emerge between high and low ethnics. High ethnics feel it is much more important that they live in an area in which there are other Japanese Americans. Consequently many high ethnics (especially if they have a family) feel that if offered a better job which would require moving to an area nearly devoid of Japanese

Americans, they would not accept it. The advantages high ethnics see in living in a Japanese American neighborhood are a) increased opportunities for their children to interact with and hopefully marry Japanese Americans, b) a greater sense of comfort in living with people who have the same values, beliefs and behaviors, c) a better chance of having some degree of local power and influence - as is the case in Gardena - since they do not feel they are as much a minority, d) security from prejudice on the part of nonJapanese Americans and e) easy access to businesses and organizations which cater to the particular desires of the ethnic community.

Low ethnics believe the economic opportunities are of much higher priority to them. Aside from the existence of stores selling Japanese food, low ethnics see little advantage to living in an ethnic community. They often see it as placing too many constraints on themselves as individuals. Low ethnics have lived in nonJapanese American neighborhoods and have experienced few if any problems of acceptance for themselves or their children on the part of the nonJapanese American community.

From the peak period of anti-Japanese hostilities during World War II that resulted in the wholesale incarceration of a people - citizen and foreign national alike, discrimination against Japanese Americans has steadily decreased. With the maturation of the third-generation, few can recall experiencing in recent years any "serious" prejudice on the part of the outside society. Some may have heard about discrimination directed against a Japanese American, but these tend to be isolated incidences. Unlike the situations of the Mexican Americans and Black Americans, there does not appear to be any overt, deliberate and widespread discrimination directed against the Japanese Americans.

There are still, however, some differences between high and low ethnics in terms of their perceptions of discrimination. High ethnics claim to have either personally experienced or heard about discrimination against Japanese Americans in schools somewhat more than low ethnics. This discrimination in schools generally revolves around the subject of quotas: Japanese Americans feel that minority admission quotas for universities and professional schools have at times hampered them. If the number of spaces available are limited by race, because of the relatively large proportion of qualified Japanese American candidates some deserving students will suffer. However, with the exception of "minor discrimination" in their personal lives, few high or low ethnics feel that they personally have experienced discrimination in terms of housing, jobs, education or in the form of police brutality.

As for discrimination in personal life, 40% of the sample feel they or a family member have experienced it, but it tends to be fairly minor - such as a child being called by a derogatory term. High ethnics also are more likely to feel that their being Japanese American is both more of a hinderence and an advantage, although only 22% of the sample feel that being Japanese American has somewhat or very badly hindered them. Fifty percent feel it is somewhat or very much of an advantage.

It is also interesting to note that while 68% of the sample disagree with the statement "Although caucasians may accept Japanese Americans in business dealings and work situations, in general they prefer not to mix with Japanese Americans socially," 64% agree that "Although Japanese Americans may accept caucasians in business dealings and work situations, in general they prefer not to mix with caucasians socially." High ethnics tend to agree with this latter statement more while low ethnics are evenly divided between agreeing and disagreeing. In general, Japanese Americans seem to feel that Japanese Americans discriminate more than are themselves discriminated against. For the high ethnics, ethnicity is by choice rather than out of necessity. (Appendix A, Table 6).

SUMMARY

Within an ethnic category - in this case all those of Japanese American ancestry - differences in a desire to be with other members of this category, i.e. to be ethnic, can and do exist. Japanese American high ethnics of the later generations differ from the low ethnics in that they have a stronger psychological identification as Japanese Americans, are more likely to see more differences between themselves as Japanese Americans and the rest of American society, take part in more activities that bring them into contact mainly with Japanese Americans while limiting the presence of nonJapanese Americans, are more concerned that their children remain ethnic, place a greater importance in living with other Japanese Americans, and are somewhat more likely to have experienced, or at least perceive they have experienced, some display of discrimination. The existence of these differences within an ethnic category does not necessarily indicate the gradual loss of ethnicity, or that those to whom ethnicity is salient are merely a dying remnant and stubborn holdouts from the inevitable assimilation into American society. In the more hospitable environment that Japanese Americans at present find themselves - little discrimination, good knowledge of American culture due to a three generation removal from Japan, fairly rapid educational, social and economic success and admiration on the part of the larger society for their attainments - they perhaps have more choices to select from and more security to follow their individual desires than did their parents and grandparents. While to all appearances it actually seems easier to assimilate, it is significant that there are Japanese Americans who wish to and are willing to make efforts necessary to separate at least a portion of their lives from the mainstream society. Why they wish to do so will be further explored in the following section.

WHY DOES ETHNICITY PERSIST FOR LATER GENERATIONS?

It is easy to understand why ethnicity plays an important role in the lives of the immigrant generation. Ethnic organizations provide a form of insurance and a sense of security to the first-generation in a new country and a new and foreign culture, as they enter the economic and social systems, often at the lowest levels. Ethnic enclaves such as the Little Italys, the Manilatowns, the Chinatowns and Little Tokyos can act as buffer zones through which information of the new culture can be filtered at a manageable rate and in an understandable manner. These enclaves help maintain symbolic ties with the familiar and often yearned for homelands. For the immigrant, what was once "national culture" has in large part become "ethnic culture," and remains as a system he understands and can be understood in.

It is also easy to realize why ethnicity may continue to be important for the second-generation, who have been socialized in two cultures simultaneously - the culture of their parents' homeland and the culture of the land in which they were born and raised. It can be an important means of survival and protection for immigrants and their children in areas and periods of extreme discrimination. In the years prior to World War II, Japanese Americans on the Pacific coast were able to find employment in ethnic enterprises when they were unable to obtain jobs elsewhere. Ethnicity remains a prominent scheme not only when assimilation is denied the immigrants and their children by the new society, but also when it is seen as an undesirable step backward by the immigrant group. Many overseas Chinese groups in South East Asia view assimilation and the loss of ethnic networks as essentially destroying an important structural advantage they hold in obtaining valuable resources; the loss would inevitably lead to the loss of control they enjoy in segments of the economies. Because they utilize the networks emanating from the ethnic group, often they have become wealthier than the majority of the host country's population and enjoy an elite position. If, for whatever reasons, the continuation of distinctive cultural elements is important to a group in a plural society, ethnicity provides one means by which this can be accomplished.

It is less obvious why ethnicity persists for some individuals of later generations when:

a) they are several generations removed from direct contact with, and knowledge of, the culture of their ancestors' homeland;

b) they appear to be so well acculturated to their country of birth and citizenship that they are basically monocultural rather than bicultural, and would have as difficult a time adjusting to the country of their forefathers as their ancestors had in adjusting to their new country[1];

c) many of them have become well-educated, done well economically, and socially are members of the middle class;

d) they are generally well regarded and seemingly face little discrimination from the majority population, particularly in the areas of society in which they are most commonly to be found;

e) they are well integrated into all aspects of this country, taking part in the same political, economic, educational, and in many cases, religious systems, often residing and coming in close and frequent contact with members of the majority society and members of other ethnic categories;

f) the new country is as advanced or even more advanced than the old country so that assimilation into it will not be perceived as a step downward; and,

g) identification with a group based on common ancestral origin does not provide any significant advantage for obtaining particular resources.

This, of course, is the case of the third-generation Japanese Americans. English is their native language and few speak Japanese. Few have been to Japan. Most of them belong to one of the major sects of Protestant Christianity. For those who are Buddhist, their churches resemble American Christian churches more than Japanese Buddhist temples. They hold Sunday services for the entire congregation, have Sunday school classes and activities for the children, have English-speaking ministers and sing hymns like "Buddha loves me this I know, because the sutra tells me so" to the accompaniment of an organ. Some *sansei* take classes in *karate* or *judo* (popular activities with the majority society as well) but many also participate in the more American sports of baseball, basketball, volleyball, golf and tennis and they avidly follow professional sports. They take part in all the major American holidays - Thanksgiving, Christmas (even the Buddhists), New Year's, Easter and the Fourth of July - with all the attendant American customs from Christmas trees to turkey and stuffing to fireworks and picnics. Most have been educated in the public school system where they have interacted with nonJapanese American classmates and teachers. Aside from a greater consumption of rice, their diet is neither extremely exotic nor different from the diet of the general American public. One of the complaints that grandparents and parents who reside with their children has been that they have trouble eating meals with the family since the meals tend to be "too American" and too heavy in oil and meat. Their children may well prefer pizza or hamburgers to fish and rice for dinner. The *issei* grandparents may have been gardeners, truck farmers or run small one-man businesses, but the *nisei* parents and the *sansei* with their increased educational attainments and greater employment opportunities, have moved into such areas as engineering, medicine, teaching, social work, law, architecture and the like, and into large nonJapanese American owned companies where ethnic contacts are of minimal benefit.

And yet, for at least some members of the third- and fourth-generations, ethnicity remains. The question is why, given their situation, are they still ethnic? Why are these people willing, if necessary, to sacrifice economic and professional advancement to remain with their own kind? Why are some willing to make the efforts to establish and extend ethnic networks when it is often more convenient not to? Some have suggested it is because ethnicity provides political and economic benefits; others have said it is because traditional cultural differences continue to exist. Neither of these seem to be major reasons in the case of the third-generation Japanese Americans. Rather the major reason here seems to be one of comfort - comfort in knowing the rules of the game, and the style in which it is carried out.

ETHNIC GROUPS AS POLITICAL AND ECONOMIC INTEREST GROUPS

Some interest groups organized on the basis of ethnic categories have been able to achieve economic and social benefits in the form of local, state and federal aid and programs directed specifically at that ethnic group. For instance, through the lobbying and demonstrations of Mexican American groups in California, all ballots and all signs in public buildings must be printed in both English and Spanish, chicano studies programs are offered in various colleges and through the impetus of minority hiring programs, Mexican Americans frequently find they have an advantage over their white colleagues. Even though America is traditionally seen as a Christian country, through the efforts of Jewish American lobbies, the potential of support from Jewish American voters, and the contribution of Jewish American dollars the federal government of the United States has been influenced in its policies toward Israel, a Jewish state. Cohen (1974:xxii) feels that "If in a dynamic contemporary complex society a group of second and third generation migrants preserve their distinctiveness and make extensive use of the symbolism of their endoculture, then the likelihood that within the contemporary situation they have become an interest group is very strong." For interest groups that for whatever reason are unable to organize themselves formally on some other basis, the use of ethnicity in "articulating the organizational functions of interest groups" can be effective (Cohen 1974:xviii).

Certainly, some members of Japanese American ethnic groups have attempted to organize in ethnically based interest groups such as the Japanese American Democrats, and the Japanese American Republicans, and a Japanese American politician can often count on the Japanese American vote. Except on a local level in an area that is strongly Japanese American in composition, such as Gardena or Monterey Park, the Japanese American population is far too small to have the type of political impact that a strong Mexican American or Black American voting block can have. A Japanese American with larger political aspirations must of necessity turn to outside non-ethnic sources of support if he is to succeed.

This lack of numbers is acknowledged by both the Japanese Americans, who are committed to the more traditional political system, as well as the more activist and politically radical Japanese Americans. Consequently, there has been a rise in programs and organizations that are composed of and directed towards an Asian American or even a larger pan-Asian Pacific Island population. Even in these cases, the numbers do not approach those of the black and hispanic populations. Furthermore, this type of organization is not "natural", and is often fraught with difficulties. Its grouping is contrived, composed of both foreign born and several generations of American born peoples from such diverse cultural backgrounds as Japanese, Korean, Chinese, Vietnamese, Samoan, Philippino, Hawaiian and others. With differing cultural and historical backgrounds, patterns of behavior and degrees of acculturation, there is less unity and more potential sources of discord and cleavage than might be found in a more "naturally" occurring ethnic group.

There was an attempt made in the late 1960s, mainly by the more politically radical and activist college age *sansei* to form a Japanese American or Asian American interest group which was to be the Yellow Power counterpart of the militant Black Power and Chicano Power movements. However, it was not very successful and presently is all but defunct. As Maykovich (1972, 1973) found in her studies of college age California *sansei*, most tend to conform to traditional Japanese American values of diligence, conformity and assimilation. Consequently, they are not actively involved in social issues, particularly those that seek a revolutionary resolution to problems. Many *sansei* have found that in the present favorable environment in which they live, they have been able to progress economically and occupationally through their own individual efforts without the need for social action programs.

PSYCHOLOGICAL AND PERSONAL BENEFITS OF ETHNICITY

The high ethnics in this study feel there are advantages to ethnicity, but they are not those leading to any economic, social or political gain. The benefits they see are the more psychological ones of a sense of comfort in being with people like themselves and a sense of security in knowing that in crisis situations there is a readily available and dependable support system of sympathetic, concerned people who will help to meet the daily demands of living while the crisis is being resolved.

There are some Japanese American individuals who feel they can interact successfully with either the ethnic community or the outside society, but have chosen to be far more involved with Japanese Americans because of the personal advantages they feel they can gain. An individual with abilities that are not usually found in the Japanese American community can, if he also understands the norms of the community and tempers his abilities accordingly, stand out in this smaller group. A Japanese American who is larger than the Japanese American norm, although perhaps of more average size among caucasians, has a greater opportunity to be outstanding in sports in the Japanese American community. An individual with an outgoing and gregarious personality may only blend in with the other outgoing personalities found in the mainstream society, but may be admired in the ethnic community where many feel such abilities are lacking.

More important, however, seems to be the *sansei* awareness of the existence of cultural differences between themselves and nonJapanese Americans and the use of a Japanese American style of coping with life situations. These factors will be discussed in the following sections.

CULTURAL DIFFERENCES

As stated above, the political-economic interest group type of ethnic solidarity does not seem to be of much relevance for many of the high ethnics studied here. Their allegiance is to Japanese Americans and not to Asian Americans or Asian/Pacific Island Americans. Their social relations with nonJapanese Americans are far more likely to be with caucasians than with other racial or subcultural groups. An important reason for the existence of ethnicity for these members of the third-generation is the fact that despite the apparent high level of acculturation and value compatibility with American culture (Caudill 1952; Caudill and Devos 1956; Kitano 1962), differences do continue to exist between Japanese Americans and other Americans. At the very least, it is so perceived by the high ethnics.

Many of these differences were described in some detail in the preceding chapter. It should be emphasized again that these differences are not necessarily differences between Americans and Japanese, but rather, are differences between Americans and Japanese Americans. Furthermore, these are not thought by the informants to be tangible ones, such as differences in language, dress, diet or religion, but are the more intangible ones of values, beliefs and behavior. Finally, the differences are important to high ethnics; they affect their lives. The high ethnics prefer in their personal and social lives to be with other Japanese Americans who are not different from themselves in these ways. Low ethnics, on the other hand, appear to be less aware of differences between themselves as Japanese Americans and the rest of American society. What differences they are aware of seem to bother them less. Where high ethnics usually see these differences as stemming from cultural sources, low ethnics are more likely to wonder if the differences they observe are due to their own idiosyncrasies. To put it simply, and perhaps simplistically, high ethnics say "I'm different because I'm Japanese American," while low ethnics say "If I am different it's because I'm me."

ETHNIC STYLE

It appears that one important factor, perhaps the crucial one, for the continuance of ethnicity for later generations of a well acculturated and integrated immigrant group is that of ethnic style. Ethnic style is not the specific things that an individual does, e.g., speak Japanese, eat with chopsticks, etc., which are often used as ethnic markers or symbols, but here is meant to be the distinctive way or flair with which an individual deals with the world, especially in regards to relating to people. It is ethnic when the whole complex of behaviors is held and understood by members of an ethnic group to be unique to themselves. It is, in essence, the unspoken, taken-for-granted, and often times very subtle rules of behavior and attendant expectations that members of the ethnic group share with each other and not with the outside society. And precisely because these rules are usually unspoken, taken-for-granted and subtle the participants are often not consciously aware of their presence. They often find it difficult to point them out. They are, however, very much aware of their absence and in their absence can become uncomfortable - "I don't know what it is, but he doesn't act right; he's not one of us."

Ethnic style is learned, not something that everyone of Japanese American ancestry is born with. It is understood by members of the community that unless their children have close contact with other Japanese Americans they will not learn it and will, therefore, be unable to fit in with and be accepted by the more ethnic Japanese Americans without modifying their behavior to fit the constraints of the Japanese American style. This style is not something that is consciously taught and cannot be learned except through interaction with Japanese Americans. Consequently, if an individual relates mainly with caucasians he will learn a different way of coping, of interacting, which is of utility in the outside society, but can run counter to the norms of the ethnic community.

Elements of the Japanese American Style

One of the things informants found hardest to do was to elucidate the specific factors that go into the makeup of the Japanese American style. Nevertheless, high ethnics are strong in their agreement that such a style exists. In discussing one element of style, for example, they stated that there are basically two types of "agreement" - one in which the individual says "yes" and agrees with what another is saying, and the other in which the individual says "yes" but disagrees with the other person. They were able to tell the difference, but found it extremely difficult to explain it to an outsider.

During the course of the research, however, certain differences in style between high ethnic Japanese Americans and the outside society did become clear. A discussion of some of the elements of the Japanese American style will help to explain the persistence of ethnicity for those of later generations.

Sensitivity to the Feelings of Others.

As a group, high ethnics are less aggressive, less assertive individuals than they find their caucasian peers to be. In general, aggressiveness is not seen as a positive trait. To the contrary, high ethnics feel that they are far more concerned with, and sensitive to, the feelings of others. They prefer to elicit the opinions and feelings of the other members of the group they are in, rather than to boldly state their own desires. They work to arrive at some sort of group consensus. In any sort of interaction there is a longer period of feeling out ("what do you want to do?" - "I don't know, what do you want to do?" and so on) than would be the norm in outside society. Suggestions are put forth more hesitantly and more as vague comments rather than firm statements of desire (There's a good movie playing at the Strand" is proper, "I want to see Superman" is less proper). Furthermore, an individual does not attempt to push his desires on the rest of the group, but waits to hear the reaction to the gentle suggestions. If the suggestion is not seen as amenable to all, they will not embarrass the person who made the suggestion by directly rejecting it (as they feel caucasians will). Instead, they will indirectly veto it by not commenting on it and offering alternatives, or by agreeing in a way that suggests a lack of enthusiasm. For instance, if a movie is suggested that someone really doesn't want to see, his response is "That's okay" which may indicate agreement to a nonJapanese American but to a Japanese American shows polite disagreement. In this way, a Japanese American expresses his opinion without running the risk of embarrassing others. Even in more formal organizational meetings there is often a greater effort made to obtain group consensus, at least on the surface; issues are not put to a vote until, through a period of group discussion, a decision is tacitly arrived at and the vote, in essence, becomes a rubber stamp approval. Those who are strongly opposed, finding themselves in the minority during the discussion period, will vote in agreement with the majority although privately, with their friends, they may complain bitterly about the decision.

Saving Face

Because the Japanese American style requires a sensitivity to the feelings and thoughts of others with whom one is in interaction, there is also stress placed on saving face, on always trying to structure one's interaction patterns so as to give other people a graceful way out. Consequently, they feel that a disagreement between Japanese Americans stemming from a difference of opinion would not be pushed as far as it would be in an argument between caucasians. They feel that caucasians try to totally destroy the arguments of their opponent, and enjoy doing it, in an attempt to prove the correctness of their opinion and to win the opposing party over to their viewpoint. A Japanese American, on the other hand, brings the disagreement to a more graceful termination by saying, whether he is convinced or not, "Well, you may be right." In this way neither person is embarrassed by being made to look foolish, and harmonious relationships are maintained.

Even in the extending of invitations to a social event, care must be taken so as to give the person invited a graceful way to refuse. To invite an individual with the words "Would you like to come . . ." places him, according to Japanese American rules of behavior, in an uncomfortable position, for if he refuses it might appear as though he doesn't want to come, thereby hurting the feelings of the host. However, by prefacing the invitation with the words "If you have the time would you like to come . . .", the invitation can be politely refused, offering as the reason the excuse suggested by the host - the implication being that if it weren't for a previously made engagement the person would have loved to attend.[2]

Avoidance of Confrontation

High ethnic Japanese Americans also feel that at least verbally they are less facile than their caucasian peers. Males, particularly, have difficulty disclosing their feelings. In extreme cases, it appears as if they are attempting to follow some idealized model of what they believe to be a part of their heritage - that of the silent, stoic *samurai* warriors. These Japanese Americans often try at all costs to avoid any sort of open conflict, particularly if they wish to maintain a relationship. Although perhaps somewhat extremely stated, the Japanese American attitude may be characterized as one of "Let's ignore it and maybe it will go away." If despite their efforts a problem in human relations develops, rather than directly dealing with it or discussing it with the parties involved, these *sansei* prefer to let it lie for a while and hope that time will heal all wounds, or failing that, put an end to a no longer workable relationship.

The resolution of a troubled relationship is a delicate, subtle and indirect process since Japanese Americans feel they lack the ability to express themselves in sensitive situations. If an individual dislikes what another person has done he never directly states that anything is wrong, much less what is wrong. Instead, he acts upset according to proper Japanese American standards - he stops talking with the individual or becomes more formal and distant in his manner - and in this way the guilty party knows something is wrong but not necessarily what. It is improper for the guilty party to confront an upset individual by asking him directly why he is angry because the injured party loses face by having to admit to his anger. In any case, the injured party will only deny that anything is wrong. The acceptable way to approach solving this problem is for the individual to think back over his past actions until he figures out what he did wrong. Then, if the injured party has not already taken the initiative in resuming the relationship as if nothing has happened (in this way he is indicating he is willing to forgive and forget), the guilty individual, if he desires to continue the relationship, must apologize for his past behavior. The matter, however, does not end here. At this point the injured party can not simply accept the apology but must politely deny any need for an apology since he had already forgotten about the incident (even though he had not). On it goes, one side tendering his apology while the other side denies the need for one, thereby saving face for both and presenting a smooth, harmonious surface to the world.

Etiquette and Formality

Sansei also feel they are more courteous and polite, particularly in formal situations, than their nonJapanese American peers seem to be. Unless they are in an informal friendship contact, they appear to feel more comfortable if the situation is more structured, where they can follow the correct rituals of social intercourse. They often note that Japanese Americans are proper and formal and are so for a longer period of time and over a wider range of situations than many nonJapanese Americans. They feel nonJapanese Americans, on the other hand, are friendlier and more outgoing and are, in this way, able to much more quickly bring the level of interaction down to a more informal and closer one. NonJapanese Americans are frequently admired for this skill but they are also criticized by Japanese Americans for what they feel to be a lack of consideration and manners.

Enryo, which the *sansei* take to mean a holding back of the expression of one's desires so as not to cause inconvenience to anyone, is still very much a part of their dealings with others. Especially in formal situations or when visiting for the first time, *sansei* feel it is good manners to politely refuse the first few times hospitality is offered them, just as the Japanese American host knows it is good manners to continue to urge hospitality on them. Consequently, when they are offered food they will at first turn it down, even though they may want it. The rationale is that even though a host offers, it will still cause him some inconvenience (he has to prepare and serve it). The host meanwhile periodically renews his offer, adding assurances that it's no trouble, and soon the guest agrees. This particular ritual of social intercourse functions properly if both parties know their roles. However, *sansei* can relate humorous anecdotes of visiting nonJapanese Americans and being offered refreshment; they politely refused the first time with the expectation that the offer would be renewed, only to find that the nonJapanese American host, being used to different rules, took the refusal as a definite one and did not offer refreshment again during the visit. A common phrase used by the Japanese American host in showing his guests hospitality is "Please don't *enryo*." However, if the guest fails to *enryo* he is seen as rude and boorish.

Group Orientation and Conformity

When compared to their caucasian peers, high ethnic Japanese Americans appear to be less individualistic. They feel more comfortable being part of a group, particularly a group of close friends. Even in high school and college these Japanese Americans enjoy socializing or dating in mixed groups rather than in individual couples as nonJapanese Americans do. Because they form closely knit friendship cliques and because of the value placed on sensitivity to the feelings of others, they are very susceptible to peer group pressure. Rather than go contrary to the wishes of the other members of the group, the individual will conform. Rather than do something alone that he prefers, a Japanese American does what his crowd does, even if he himself is not enthusiastic about it. This desire to conform to the group is established early in childhood. Mothers ask their children what their friends are doing or buy them what their group or community deems to be currently fashionable in clothing - they don't want their children to be different from their friends.

It is acknowledged that due to this emphasis placed on group conformity, high ethnic Japanese Americans tend to be less tolerant of individual differences than they feel nonJapanese Americans are.

Social control is tight but is accomplished in an indirect and nonconfronting fashion. For minor transgressions displeasure is expressed through body language rather than through a direct verbal statement. Through a hurt or somewhat angry look, silence, or a physical drawing back, one feels rather than hears the displeasure. Then efforts are quickly made by the knowledgeable party to modify his behavior. For larger offenses social control is brought to bear through the use of ridicule and ostracism. These methods are usually performed by a group. They may "politely" ignore the transgressor, being so involved in other conversations or activities that they fail to acknowledge his presence. It is, in essence, a means by which a group can confront without being confronting. This type of treatment is so painful to a Japanese American who is aware of and cares about the opinions of his group that he will either modify his behavior if he can or will terminate his relationship with the group. In either case group homogeneity is maintained.

The Japanese American style does not make for easy intercourse in unfamiliar and less structured situations. It is difficult for a Japanese American to be a total stranger in any situation for it is not usually considered proper to interact informally with someone unless he has been introduced by a mutual friend or acquaintance. Furthermore, Japanese Americans are accustomed to and prefer to interact as a member of a group rather than as individuals and so need to know the people they are interacting with before they can feel comfortable with them. As a result, before a Japanese American attends a social event he wants to ascertain if he knows enough of the other guests. If, after the host invites him with, "If you have the time I was wondering if you would like to come to a party?" the host fails to mention the names of other guests that he might know, it is considered proper to ask "Who is coming?". If the person being invited knows enough of the guests he'll come and if he doesn't he won't have the time. Japanese Americans are also avid players of the "do you know?" game, whether they have been properly introduced or are strangers who find it necessary to interact (one can only sit in silence for so long when at a common dining table). The object of this game is to attempt to find a mutual friend or acquaintance. In this way the players can feel closer to each other through this link. Because ethnic networks are important and are extensive, because the Japanese American population in relation to the rest of the U.S. population is quite small, and because the various Japanese American communities are both close knit and interrelated, informants report a high degree of success in finding mutual acquaintances.

Generosity and Reciprocal Obligation

As has been previously discussed, reciprocal obligation and generosity are very important values among *sansei*, and as such they are important components of the Japanese American style. According to the prevailing norm it is expected that one always fights for the dinner check but no one in a group constantly ends up paying for everyone. There is always the underlying awareness of the obligation to repay what one has received, and a consequent careful, though unspoken accounting of each person's social debits and credits. The generosity exhibited by high ethnic *sansei* may seem spontaneous, casual and with no attendant obligations, for they are embarrassed and impatient with nickel-and-dime quibbling over checks, but there is an expectation that the other Japanese Americans will be equally generous. Housewives drew a distinction between Japanese Americans and nonJapanese Americans in the following terms - a nonJapanese American family will see nothing wrong in bringing a salad to a potluck dinner while a Japanese American family, not wanting to take a "free-ride" on the generosity of others, will bring two types of food, one of which is often a meat dish, the most expensive part of a meal. High ethnics as a result don't like to potluck with nonJapanese Americans for they feel their obligatory generosity is being taken advantage of.

Because the obligation to reciprocate and to do so generously is such a compelling norm, which is strengthened by the Japanese American concern about other people's opinions, obligation never has to be openly stated or pointed out and, in fact, to do so is seen as extremely rude. It is, in this case, to confront an individual with what he already knows he needs to do. It does not carry a stigma with nonJapanese Americans, however, and their habit of saying "You owe me a favor," or "I owe you one," is extremely distasteful to Japanese Americans and causes them discomfort when it occurs in their dealings with the outside society.

Importance of Style

An awareness, an understanding and proper use of the Japanese American style is so important that the lack of it in a *sansei* will cause him to be ostracized by his Japanese American peers. The presence of it in a nonJapanese American, which is rare, will on occasion permit him to be accepted by the ethnic community. In Gardena and various other Japanese American communities and organizations in the Los Angeles and Orange county areas there are those nonJapanese Americans, particularly caucasian males, who for reasons of their own are very much attracted to various aspects of Japanese culture or the Japanese American community. They will attend Japanese American churches, go to various Japanese American social and cultural events, take classes in martial arts or Japanese language, date mainly Asian females, and feel that in this way they are well accepted by the Japanese Americans. Most seem to be misfits in their own culture who romantically yearn to be part of another culture. And yet, misfits in their own culture, they are usually misfits in the Japanese American culture, for few of them appear to have enough awareness of the art of human relations to have learned to deal with people according to Japanese American norms. Seemingly politely received by the community, little do these "ethnic" nonJapanese Americans realize that behind their back they are being ridiculed and viewed with resentment. There is a rare type of caucasian however who gets along very well with Japanese Americans. Usually these individuals display the same type of characteristics as do the high ethnic Japanese Americans - they are less aggressive, less confronting, more polite and more sensitive to the feelings of others and are more understanding and tolerant of the way their Japanese American friends may deal with particular situations. In essence, they display a personal style of coping with life situations which is more akin to the Japanese American one than it is to the mainstream style. They are amenable to further behavior modification, if necessary, in order to better fit into the Japanese American community. As a result, the major portion of their social lives is spent with Japanese Americans.

Generally, the Japanese American style is one that is learned gradually and unconsciously in childhood through interaction with other Japanese Americans. Many of them may have learned only one pattern of behavior, since their relations with nonJapanese Americans tend to be limited, impersonal, formal and highly structured ones, e.g. professor and student, businessperson and client. As a result, they feel uncomfortable in nonJapanese American situations for they are in a different game where the rules they have learned and are used to playing by no longer hold and the unspoken expectations they have are not met. Furthermore, dealing with people in the only way they know how, they often feel they are at a disadvantage when they, with their Japanese American style must deal with an individual with a nonJapanese American style.

There are those who learn one ethnic style in childhood and adolescence. In adulthood, however, they learn an alternate one out of a desire to become more or less ethnic or in order to better cope in their occupation in the larger nonJapanese American world. Most of them have found that it is difficult to continually switch styles depending on the situation they find themselves in, or to switch to a previously learned style after an intensive period of usage of another style. This is particularly so the more they find themselves interacting with Japanese Americans.

Unless there is some compelling reason such as an extreme amount of discrimination on the part of the mainstream society, it is usually easier for an individual to interact with people who display the same style of human relations that he feels most comfortable with and most skillful at. In terms of daily and close, personal relations, he prefers to be with his "own kind." This "kind", however, is based less on a criterion of race or descent from an ancestral cultural group category than on commonly understood and shared rules of behavior in the area of human relations. Consequently, *sansei* will exclude from membership other *sansei* who do not behave as they do, and will include the few nonJapanese Americans who are able to understand and display all the complex nuances of the *sansei* ethnic style.

The Clan: A Case Study in Style Conflict

The following case study is an example of some elements of the Japanese American style, the conflict that can result when deviance occurs, and the Japanese American way of dealing with this conflict.

The Clan is a club of six families, of which most of the men were childhood friends. Originating from Los Angeles county the young couples who were just beginning their families had gotten together socially on one occasion and had so enjoyed it that they continued to do so. They soon decided to organize into a more structured club with elected officers, dues and planned activities. Club activities are geared around the children, and the purpose is to give the entire families a chance to socialize. In addition to meetings and four major club events each year - usually a Halloween Party, a Christmas or New Year's Party, a camping trip or beach party and an excursion to another city - when they lived closer together and their children were younger much informal socializing of the club members also occurred at birthday parties and so on. Activities as a club are more limited now due to the scattering of the families within Los Angeles and Orange counties, and due to the increased involvement of their children in other organizations which leaves them less available time for the club. However, individual members continue to socialize with each other.

The adult members are presently in their mid-30's and all are second- or third-generation Japanese American except for the wife of one member. It is felt by some of the other females in the club that this nonJapanese American member has been the source of conflict over money because her ways are different. As was previously indicated, among high ethnic Japanese Americans a show of generosity, especially when dealing with one's friends, is very important. To quibble over small amounts of money is distasteful to them. It was noticed with disapproval that whereas the Japanese American members purchase with their own money supplies such as stamps to mail out club letters, etc. for club business and do not expect nor want to be reimbursed, the nonJapanese American member requests repayment for every item she buys for club activities, regardless of how small the amount.

Last year, a crisis arose in the club because of the actions of Sharon, the nonJapanese American member. During the year dues are collected to help defray the cost of the one big field trip the club takes each year. That year the club decided to go to San Francisco for the weekend. Due to the business connections of one member, the club was able to obtain lodgings at a considerable discount. But because Sharon had brought her sister and a friend along, as well as using room service, the total bill was over the amount collected in dues. Consequently, everyone had to contribute additional funds. The understanding in the club had been that nonmembers could be invited but the host family was then supposed to cover any additional expense over what was collected in dues. Furthermore, in the evening the adults went out while the children were watched by babysitters who are the nonpaying guests. It was expected that they were to babysit as partial payment for the trip - i.e. reciprocal obligation - and therefore were not to expect any reimbursement for their services. Another member had also brought her sister, who babysat along with Sharon's sister. The Japanese American babysitter didn't expect or request payment for babysitting, but Sharon, the nonJapanese American member, wanted each family to pay her sister five dollars. A further source of anger for the rest of the club was that Sharon had brought some food which she also asked to be reimbursed for since the food was to be for the entire club. She kept it in her family's hotel room, however, necessitating a trip to that room. Relationships between Sharon and the rest of the club had deteriorated by then and few felt like going to Sharon's room. Consequently, the food was mostly consumed by Sharon and her family. It was felt that a Japanese American would usually not ask to be reimbursed unless it was a considerable expense, would have been taken care that the food was easily accessible to all and, if the family purchasing the food had consumed most of it, would not have wanted repayment regardless of prior arrangements.

All the club members were very upset with the behavior of Sharon and discussed it angrily among themselves. But they would not confront Sharon about it. Linda suggested that Ellen talk gently with Sharon since the two families lived in the same area and Ellen was the closest of the group to Sharon. But Ellen refused, _in fear of hurting Sharon's feelings_, despite the anger of the entire group towards Sharon and the threat it posed to the continued harmonious functioning of the club.

Sharon eventually became aware that for some reason the members of the club were upset with her. It occurred in an indirect manner. The next planning meeting for the club was to be held at Sharon's house; she was the hostess and was responsible for supplying refreshments. At the last minute, after all her preparations for the evening had been completed, everyone cancelled out of the meeting. In this way, no one ever directly confronted Sharon, but through their actions it was let known to her that she had erred. She was not exactly certain as to what she had done wrong but club members noticed that since that trip she had become more reserved in her behavior in an attempt to avoid further hurting peoples' feelings. It was noted by one informant that if this had happened to a Japanese American, she would have known enough to think back to the last occasion before the concerned individuals began to act "strangely" in their behavior towards her, review her own actions and try to figure out what she did wrong to cause people to become upset.

Because Sharon is not Japanese American she is not totally familiar with, skillful in, nor willing to modify her behavior to fit the Japanese American style. As a result, she has unintentionally caused some turmoil in the club and, puzzled by the reactions of the Japanese American members feels, at times, that she would like to dropout. Certainly, it was only because she had married a Japanese American who has maintained his friendships with several Japanese American classmates that she had been included in this ethnically composed organization in the first place. One couple who are less ethnically oriented than many of the other members have tried to widen club membership to include nonJapanese American families but, to date, all such attempts have failed. The nonJapanese Americans who have been invited in seem to be less involved, attend fewer events, and eventually completely drop out, and the rest of the Japanese American members are not enthusiastic about inviting others. Most likely the nonJapanese Americans, without knowing what it is exactly, simply feel different, that they don't belong, and are, therefore, less comfortable. They do not share the same style as the Japanese Americans and find socializing with high ethnic Japanese Americans somewhat puzzling and less enjoyable.

SUMMARY

The type of ethnicity that exists today among high ethnic *sansei* can be seen perhaps as a more "natural" and traditional type of ethnicity in that one lives it rather than uses it strategically for political or economic manipulation and gain. These *sansei* are ethnic because they perceive the existence of cultural differences that set them apart from the mainstream society. It should be noted that these cultural differences are not necessarily Japanese[3] in nature; high ethnics feel far more different in manner and behavior from Japanese nationals than from mainstream Americans. Some may go to Japan seeking their roots, but they return realizing that they have been American tourists. The differences that exist may well be unique to the Japanese Americans and their historical experiences in America. It should also be noted that the differences cited by high ethnics are not of the "quaint customs, archaic survivals and material culture" school, for they see the significant differences to lie in the area of values, norms and rules of behavior in interpersonal relations. These are far more compelling reasons to remain in some part separate from the larger society, but these are also differences that are far more difficult to consciously delineate, especially by an outsider. It is easy to point out that this group sometimes uses chopsticks while that group always uses forks, but more difficult to point out differences in their sense of obligation to reciprocate for every favor received.

Stemming from cultural differences comes the very important factor of ethnic style - the way in which individuals negotiate their human relations according to ethnically defined patterns or rules of behavior. The difference in style between a high ethnic Japanese American and a nonJapanese American may be very subtle but very complex, and contribute much to the feeling of comfort with one's "own kind" and discomfort with those who are not of one's "own kind." A sense of comfort may be unexciting as an explanation for the continued existence of ethnicity among later generations but it is important. In order to succeed economically, politically or socially, individuals may be willing to tolerate a good deal of difference, but in at least the personal and noninstrumental portions of their lives, many want to be able to relax and feel comfortable knowing they are among people with the same expectations and behavior as they.

Finally, there are individuals who have consciously opted for ethnicity because of the personal benefits they feel they can gain. In the smaller, more tightly enmeshed ethnic community individuals with particular abilities that are admired but lacking in this group can carve a niche for themselves, whereas in the larger society it is more likely they would be lost in the crowd. However, their abilities are only accepted by the ethnic community if the individual in question tailors them to fit into the ethnic style of the community.

HOW IS ETHNICITY MAINTAINED?

Given that many later generation Japanese Americans choose to interact in their personal and social lives mainly with other Japanese Americans - i.e., to be ethnic, attention must be turned to the problem of how ethnic relations are established and maintained. How does a *sansei* meet and establish friendships with Japanese Americans while at the same time excluding nonJapanese Americans from participating in his social life?

This question is especially interesting in light of the particular situation of the *sansei*. He lives in a neighborhood with at least some nonJapanese American families, attends public school and college with nonJapanese Americans and works in a nonJapanese American owned company with nonJapanese American co-workers and a nonJapanese boss. He speaks only English, likes hot dogs and pizza, is an avid follower of college and professional football and baseball, goes to the movies or to dances on Friday nights, plays golf or bowls on Saturdays and goes to church on Sundays. He has found that few if any areas of the mainstream society are barred to him. Most of his peers have never personally experienced any form of prejudice. Few of them went through the Japanese American relocation/concentration camp experience during World War II. Many of those who did were too young at the time to remember details of it. To many of them it is an event of mainly historical importance and does not carry the emotional impact that memories of the Holocaust have for Jews of today.

In sum, the *sansei* are highly acculturated, face little if any discrimination and as a group have done extremely well educationally, occupationally and economically. In such a favorable environment and under such favorable conditions how do high ethnic *sansei* maintain the "ethnic purity" of their lives?

A person is not born ethnic although he may be born into an ethnic environment; his parents may be high ethnics and live in an ethnically homogeneous neighborhood. This can facilitate the process of his becoming ethnic. Becoming ethnic is a two part process. To be high ethnic, he needs to learn the appropriate behavior to be accepted by his fellow ethnics. Secondly, he needs to establish, intensify and widen networks of social relations with other high ethnic Japanese Americans. The first part - the learning of ethnic behavior, values, perception, etc. - is not necessarily accomplished through a deliberate or conscious effort, but may simply result from enculturation. For those raised by high ethnic parents and among high ethnic peers, it is a simple and natural process. For those not raised in an ethnic environment but later consciously choosing to become ethnic, it is often a difficult and complex process at which they may not succeed. In essence, it requires a "reprogramming" of behavioral and relational patterns, a modification of their previous spontaneous behavior.

Regardless of the effort required, each individual must be able to fit into the ethnic group in a way comfortable for all - otherwise he will be rejected by the other members. Similarly, an individual who has been raised in the ways of the ethnic community but has chosen to become less ethnic, must learn and adjust to the new ways of the mainstream society.

Ethnicity as it is defined here is a type of social or group behavior. It cannot exist in isolation. It must be carried out with other people of the same ethnic category as oneself. Consequently, to be high ethnic, it is crucial for not only to learn and display the appropriate behavior of the ethnic group, but also to establish relationships with other members of the ethnic group. This chapter discusses how Japanese American ethnic networks are established, intensified and extended in an area in which there is at least some degree of Japanese American residential concentration. The following chapter deals with the establishment of ethnic networks in an area lacking such a residential concentration. While the environmental setting results in certain differences, many of the factors are similar, particularly the role of institutionalized reciprocal obligation.

FRIENDSHIP NETWORKS

The High Ethnic Family

It is well known in the Japanese American community that children who are born in high ethnic families tend to become high ethnic adults, while children born in low ethnic families, particularly in areas with few Japanese Americans, tend to become low ethnic adults.

Children of high ethnic families are socialized in an environment that is filled with Japanese American relatives and friends, all of whom are involved in the Japanese American subculture. Because of their parents' social patterns, their playmates are Japanese American. In fact, their first opportunity to form friendships with nonJapanese American children may not occur until they attend public school. Any attempt to take advantage of this opportunity can be subtly discouraged by their parents in a number of ways. High ethnic mothers will ask their children if a new-found playmate is Japanese American. In doing so, they begin to sensitize the children to the fact that there is a difference. They feel that Japanese American parents take better and more protective care of children, whereas nonJapanese American parents are more lax in their approach to child rearing[1]. They have confidence that if their children are visiting at a Japanese American friend's home, rather than at a nonJapanese American home, they will not only be well looked after, but also fed an adequate meal and even driven home if necessary. They are also less enthusiastic about nonJapanese American friends visiting their own home and less willing to inconvenience themselves to enable them to do so. Their children's only opportunity to play with nonJapanese Americans may thus occur only in the context of school situations.

As their children grow older, high ethnic parents make efforts to enroll them in after school youth activities and organizations that are totally Japanese American in membership - a Japanese American boy or girl scout troop rather than a nonJapanese American or mixed one, a Japanese American father-son club in the YMCA, a Japanese American athletic league. What free time the children have is limited even further to interaction with other Japanese American children. The block they live on may have few Japanese American children of their age group, but the children they grow up with and make friends with are mainly fellow Japanese Americans. Networks formed outside of the school environment can begin to appear in the school, as Japanese American cliques form and school sponsored service and social clubs become heavy in Japanese American members as friends invite other friends to join.

Finally, Japanese American parents often comment that their children just seem to be attracted to other Japanese Americans, they seem to have a "natural affinity for each other" and to seek each other out. This observation shouldn't be surprising - from an early age the children see their parents socialize almost exclusively with Japanese Americans, listen as their parents tell them that Japanese Americans are better, hear them complain about the behavior of nonJapanese Americans, are taught by their parents to be aware if their playmates are Japanese American or not, find it easier to obtain permission to visit Japanese Americans than nonJapanese Americans and through the efforts of their parents find themselves surrounded by potential Japanese American friends in convivial Japanese American settings.

The Formation of Ethnic Networks

It is felt by many of the informants - high, middle and low ethnics - that Japanese Americans, including *sansei*, tend to be shyer and less at ease among strangers (Japanese American or nonJapanese American) than nonJapanese Americans tend to be. They feel that in social situations nonJapanese Americans, particularly caucasians, are outgoing, are willing to converse with strangers and able to socialize with greater ease, and form more and quicker acquaintanceships and friendships than Japanese Americans are able to. Japanese Americans are more cautious when establishing friendships and once in such a relationship, they appear to take it far more seriously than they feel nonJapanese Americans do. Particularly in crisis situations it is their Japanese American friends who they can depend upon, who will respond first, to a greater extent and for a longer duration than would nonJapanese American friends.

Because they find it more difficult to interact casually with strangers, high ethnic *sansei* try to avoid social situations in which they may know few or none of the other people. It is not considered impolite to ask, when invited to a party, "Who is coming?" and then, if not enough people are attending that one already knows, to decline the invitation. High ethnics prefer to move through social situations comfortably surrounded by a network of friends. Given this situation how do Japanese Americans establish their networks?

For *sansei*, entry into a group is effected through an introduction by a mutual friend or member of the group. This makes it difficult for a newcomer since the members only welcome those who have been vouched for by means of an introduction (see also Hosokawa (1973)). This is less difficult for *sansei* who have from childhood interacted with other Japanese Americans. They already know Japanese Americans and this population is small enough and the ethnic communities cohesive enough that people often find they have mutual acquaintances or are linked by mutual acquaintance to others. They may also see each other at the same events or places - the same carnival, the same bowling alley, the same restaurant. These *sansei* may not be close friends with everyone but they at least are familiar with a large number of people in the Japanese American community.

Entry is more difficult for Japanese Americans who either have not been raised among Japanese Americans and, as a result, have only begun to form their ethnic networks, or who are in a city that is unfamiliar to them. Once they find some previous acquaintance who can introduce them to other Japanese Americans, however, the process becomes easier as they become known to a larger and larger number of Japanese Americans, who in turn can potentially introduce them to still other Japanese Americans.

As well as extending their friendship networks, high ethnic *sansei* also work to intensify their relations with particular groups of friends. The young singles in particular, like to socialize in groups, socialize often with the same group or groups of friends, and form very tight friendships which extend into a greater portion of their lives. Some groups become so tight that it is difficult to include any new Japanese American members. Other groups consist of a tight nucleus of friends around which other mutual friends swirl in and out. This tendency of high ethnic *sansei* to socialize heavily in close knit Japanese American groups is one type of behavior that low ethnics find distasteful, labeling it as "cliquish."

There are a number of places in Los Angeles that one can go to with one's friends that have become Japanese American "territories". There are particular restaurants, nightclubs, bars and hamburger stands that Japanese Americans frequent, social dances that primarily Japanese Americans or other Asian Americans attend, there are particular floors of campus libraries or tables in school cafeterias that have become Japanese American "property", and even a particular area of a public beach to which Japanese American sunbathers and surfers come. These are all public places open to Japanese American and nonJapanese American alike, but through their regular and heavy patronage Japanese Americans have made them their own. Here they not only can socialize in comfort surrounded by other Japanese Americans (many high ethnics stated they felt self-conscious to be one of only a few Asians in an otherwise nonJapanese American group) but by going to the same places they can meet with friends and possibly be introduced to some new Japanese Americans.

For divorced Japanese Americans seeking another Japanese American partner there are particular bars with dance floors they frequent, and continue to frequent, even though they see the same people each time, none of whom may hold any romantic interest for them. It becomes a social gathering of friends. They find it very difficult to frequent different bars because 1) they would be strangers there, a situation they find extremely uncomfortable, and 2) if they attended the far more numerous nonJapanese American bars in southern California, it would mean they would have to socialize with nonJapanese Americans, something they aren't interested in doing since they are hoping to date and marry another Japanese American.

The Exclusion of NonJapanese Americans

The reliance on an introduction for admittance into a group serves to bring only Japanese Americans in, and to keep nonJapanese Americans out. Because this is a Japanese American behavior pattern, nonJapanese Americans may attempt to enter a Japanese American group but they usually do so in a manner unacceptable to the group members and, as a result, will be rebuffed from the very beginning. Furthermore, as Hosokawa (1973:210) found, since the members' present group of friends is Japanese American, and the people they each know are Japanese American, any new person they are likely to be introduced to will also be Japanese American.

There are additional unspoken norms which make it difficult for a high ethnic to bring nonJapanese Americans into his networks. Informants have said they do not include a nonJapanese American friend or date in an all Japanese American event because it would make all the Japanese Americans there uncomfortable and would make themselves feel conspicuous and therefore, also uncomfortable. They also feel that their nonJapanese American friend, unaccustomed to being in such a minority position, would also probably feel ill at ease. Since many of the activities of the groups do take place in an all Japanese American environment - Japanese American dances, Japanese American bars, Japanese American volleyball tournaments - this would limit the areas in which a high ethnic would even contemplate including nonJapanese Americans. To bring nonJapanese Americans into one's group, against group convention, requires some serious consideration on the part of the responsible individual; it is not something casually attempted.

If a group member persists in including nonJapanese Americans in ethnic group activities, and these newcomers do not fit in well (and the chances are they will not unless they are aware of and willing to behave according to the Japanese American style), the other Japanese American members will act to let their displeasure be known. They may jokingly say, "Oh, are you bringing your white friend again?", will politely ignore the newcomer or become overly formal in their actions. This type of behavior tends to be effective in bringing the straying member back into line with group norms. In fact, some informants who have invited nonJapanese American friends along with their Japanese American group report they do not reinvite the outsiders unless the group response is enthusiastic. For the stubborn individual, ostracism is the next step. Group activities are carefully arranged so as to exclude this individual and his nonJapanese American friends. He then has two choices - to conform to group norms, socializing with his nonJapanese American friends only outside of the group, or to leave his ethnic network and socialize solely with his nonJapanese American friends. Ostracism by the group usually does not need to be imposed, for if an individual is so adamant about including nonJapanese Americans that he will willingly go against the wishes of his Japanese American friends he is probably already willing to divest himself of his ethnic ties. He then leaves the group of his own volition, viewing his former friends as too narrow-minded.

With the rise in the rate of outmarriage for Japanese Americans in recent years (Kikumura and Kitano 1973; Tinker 1973), the necessity of dealing with nonJapanese Americans in *sansei* groups is on the increase. Many Japanese Americans who have outmarried, however, were never strongly attached to a Japanese American group in the first place, but rather, were directed toward the mainstream society; their marriage requires little or no adjustment for the high ethnics. However, there are high ethnics who have outmarried and this can pose a problem if they wish to continue their ethnic group affiliation. There is more acceptance on the part of Japanese

American friends when an individual's involvement with a nonJapanese American is a serious one, but the nonJapanese American spouse must still, to some degree, be able to fit into the group. Failing this, the Japanese Americans will begin to avoid socializing with this couple. Furthermore, if the nonJapanese American spouse feels uncomfortable in an all Japanese American situation, he or she will also prefer to limit his/her interactions with the group. In either case, the result is less involvement with Japanese Americans for this couple. Be he Japanese American or nonJapanese American, the individual must conform to Japanese American norms and feel comfortable in all Japanese American situations in order to be accepted into any Japanese American group.

ORGANIZATIONAL NETWORKS

Japanese American Organizations and Institutions

For many Japanese Americans who have been raised in an ethnic environment their socializing in informal Japanese American friendship groups precludes any need to participate in the more formally structured Japanese American organizations. Their social life with Japanese Americans so monopolizes their free time that they do not need to turn to ethnic organizations, such as churches or social clubs, to establish and widen their networks.

This does not mean that the Japanese American community is lacking in ethnically defined organizations. Japanese Americans, if they are joiners, have a wide range to chose from to fit their particular interests. While there are some organizations that are more uniquely Asian in nature, such as a *kendo* (Japanese sword fighting) or *judo* club, most organizations seem to parallel organizations that are to be found also in the mainstream society. There are businessmen's clubs such as the Lions, Kiwanis and Optimists that have Japanese American chapters. There are the Japanese American Republican and Democratic clubs. There are Japanese American cub scout, boy scout, brownie scout and girl scout troops. There are Japanese American athletic leagues for both sexes and all ages from elementary school on up, and a wide range of sports from softball to volleyball to golf to skiing. There are separate Veterans of Foreign Wars posts for Japanese Americans - in Gardena the Japanese American post is located two blocks away from the other VFW post in the city. There are Japanese American society women's social clubs. The list is long.

As well as ethnically separate clubs and organizations there are also separate Japanese American institutions which increase interaction between Japanese Americans and limit it with nonJapanese Americans. Japanese American Buddhist and Christian churches provide a wide range of religious and nonreligious organizations and activities for the Japanese American population. Although not officially restricted ethnically, their composition is almost entirely Japanese American.

In Gardena, as in other communities with a sizable number of Japanese Americans, there is a Japanese American community center just a few blocks from the city's community center. The Gardena Valley Japanese Cultural Institute's facilities consist of a two story building adjacent to the Japanese American VFW hall. The first floor has basically a large hall for banquets, parties and classes and a kitchen and a locker room. The second floor holds the institute's offices, classrooms and a conference room. Plans are being finalized to build a second building, a gymnasium-auditorium, with athletic facilities, a stage and a projection room. The rest of the property is used for softball and baseball.

Although supposedly open to the general public, in actuality the institute is almost completely patronized by Japanese Americans. The facilities are heavily utilized during the days, evenings, and weekends with martial arts and various Japanese cultural art lessons, adult education classes, Japanese language school, senior citizens hot meals programs for Japanese Americans, and softball tournaments. It serves as a center for various meetings and cultural events of the ethnic community. Without the existence of this ethnic community center, Japanese Americans would have had to patronize the mainstream institutions far more heavily than they presently do. Thus, the center serves as an additional area in which Japanese Americans, insulated from the presence of nonJapanese Americans, can meet on an informal basis with other Japanese Americans. It gives them the added benefit of learning something about Japanese culture.

Japanese Americans can not only separate themselves from the mainstream society through participation in distinctly Japanese American organizations and institutions, but can separate themselves even while participating in an organization that draws its membership from the entire community. The Gardena YMCA provides a case in point. Within the YMCA structure is a father-son organization called the Indian Guides, which is composed of smaller groups called tribes. The tribes are the actual functioning bodies wherein members come into close personal contact with each other. Two of the tribes are totally Japanese American in composition. As a result, the high ethnic can meet his own personal needs and interests by conducting his social life in the company of other Japanese Americans.

In structure and function, many of the ethnic organizations seem much like any voluntary organization to be found in the mainstream society. There are, however, major differences. Because high ethnic Japanese Americans feel uncomfortable among strangers, whether Japanese American or not, they tend to join a formal organization only if they already have friends in it. In Gardena, a community with a concentrated Japanese American population, individuals have been raised in an ethnic environment and have already established their networks. As a result, they do not usually join organizations to extend their networks, although this can occur. They tend, instead, to join organizations in order to intensify already existing informal networks; the organizational setting is one more arena for interaction with Japanese American friends. Thus, participation in ethnic organizations not only deepens involvement in ethnic life but also helps partition the ethnic subcommunity from the outside society.

The following description and discussion of Japanese American athletic leagues shows how one such ethnic organization functions in a Japanese American community.

Japanese American Athletic Leagues - *Sansei* League and FOR Club

In Gardena, there are two major Japanese American athletic leagues for children. Gardena FOR Junior Sports Association and Gardena Valley *Sansei* League are the ethnic counterparts of Little League or the Parks and Recreation Department athletic program. There is a rule that the players must have at least one parent of Japanese ancestry to be eligible to play in the leagues. The rationale for limiting the teams to Japanese Americans (in some other ethnic leagues a specified number of nonJapanese Americans are allowed per team) is that their smaller physical stature puts them at a disadvantage in athletic competition with nonJapanese Americans. By excluding nonJapanese Americans, their children will hopefully have more opportunities to play and to play successfully.

There are also unstated reasons for the ethnically segregated leagues. They are a means for the intensification and extension of social networks. Additionally, they provide a sense of community with other Japanese Americans which can be maintained without interference from outsiders. The Gardena Japanese Americans are proud that this is their league. They fear that if nonJapanese Americans were admitted, they would soon dominate both the leadership and the competition because of being more aggressive and confronting.

Thus, even high ethnic Japanese Americans who have the size as well as the ability to compete athletically with nonJapanese Americans prefer not to and join the Japanese American teams instead. A football coach at a local high school has tried unsuccessfully to recruit some *sansei* youths to play on the school team but has found they would rather be with their Japanese American friends. It is interesting to note that for low ethnic parents whose children competed in sports with nonJapanese Americans, size was less of a consideration. What their children might lack in size they felt was compensated for in skill or in just the enjoyment of playing.

Ethnic athletic leagues are not a new development for the Japanese American community. For the second-generation, they were a fact of life due to rising anti-Japanese sentiment in the pre-World War II years and the immediate post-War years. However, what appears to be new is the current widespread popularity of athletics for both adults and children, male and female. Although there exists an interest in Japanese martial arts, the athletic leagues focus on the same sports that are found in the mainstream society - baseball, basketball, volleyball, golf, tennis, skiing, etc. Football is the only major American sport they do not promote for their children, although watching the Rose Bowl game on New Year's Day has become almost an intrinsic part of the Japanese American New Year's celebration. The reason given for the lack of interest in playing is that football is too overtly aggressive a sport and is too dangerous since it involves a good deal of body contact.

Of the two, FOR club is the older and the larger. FOR stands for Friends of Richard and was started in 1959 as a very small group of four teams in honor of a young Japanese American who died suddenly, very shortly after being named as a starter on the local junior college's basketball team. In the mid-1960s, FOR was seen as providing a healthier alternative to the experimentation with drugs on the part of the Japanese American youth, particularly after a series of *sansei* drug-related deaths shocked the Japanese American community.

Membership in FOR club can continue through high school and even into college. At the time of this research FOR club had 50 girls' and boys' basketball teams and 38 softball and baseball teams, had sent teams to compete in Hawaii and was sending a boy's team to compete in Japan. Practice sessions are held after school in Gardena. Competition occurs on the weekends since FOR club teams compete against Japanese American teams from other cities in Los Angeles county. This involves a good deal of inconvenience on the part of the parents as they give up their weekends to transport their children to the city where a particular game is being held. This is not to mention the additional responsibilities parents assume as the officers, managers, coaches, various committee members and assistants.

Sansei League was begun because more children wanted to play on a Japanese American team than FOR club could handle. It is smaller - 26 boys and girls softball teams and about the same number of basketball teams. Unlike FOR club, competition is only within *Sansei* League; games are all held on the grounds of the Gardena Valley Japanese Cultural Institute both after school and on weekends. Participation is time consuming with twice weekly practice sessions before the season and one to two 2-hour games, plus a 2-hour practice session each week during the season. Again officials, coaches, managers and support personnel are drawn from the ranks of the parents. If a family participates in both basketball and softball, with both preseason practice and seasonal competition, only one month of the year is left free. Like FOR Club, the *Sansei* League teams are each sponsored by various Japanese American organizations in the community. Their responsibilities are to provide uniforms and equipment for each of their teams. Many organizations sponsor a number of teams and some sponsor teams in both leagues. Funds for additional expenses such as insurance, umpire fees, trophies, supplies, etc., which ran to nearly $11,000 for the 1977 season, are raised through registration fees, donations, and the sale of refreshments during the games. Currently teams only run up to the ninth grade.

Group Participation in Organizations

Joining a Japanese American athletic league is difficult for an individual, especially for the older children. FOR Club and *Sansei* League are unlike the athletic leagues found in the nonJapanese American community, where children simply try out or sign up and then are assigned to teams. Instead, groups of people get together to enter as already formed teams. Each team often consists of relatives, friends and friends-of-friends of approximately the same age, since the leagues are divided into age graded divisions. If a particular team disbands for some reason (e.g. lack of interest on too many of the members' part, or an inability on the parent's part to all get along), the remaining members of the former team are not usually distributed among the other teams. Instead, they must drop out of competition until they can find enough people to start another team.

Exceptions are made only for children with outstanding athletic ability or if there is a vacancy on another team.

Unlike Little League, teams remain together year after year rather than being reformed into new teams with different members each season. Team membership only changes when some players become too old for their division and have to move up individually. Frequently, however, the children on any one team are close enough together in age that they can move up as the same team into a new division. Alternatively, if a large enough number of players from several teams are moving up they will be formed into a completely new team in the older division.

Under this system, the children and adults do not have to deal each year with people they might not know. There is the possibility of meeting new Japanese American families, but of greater attraction is the opportunity for both parents and children to intensify relationships with familiar people. If team families get along well together, they socialize outside of athletic events and League related activities as adults, as children and as families.

This tendency to participate in organizations as groups rather than individuals is an important means by which groups can remain ethnic in composition even while part of a larger nonJapanese American structure. In the case of the YMCA and the Indian Guides, father-son couples from the two Japanese American tribes decided to join together and enter the next organizational level, the Grey Y's, as an already formed group. Thus they avoided being split up and distributed among already existing nonJapanese American groups. They continue to remain a homogeneous Japanese American group in a heterogeneous nonJapanese American organization. In addition, vacancies on the two Japanese American Indian Guide tribes are not filled by the YMCA organization. Instead, other father-son pairs are invited to join by the existing members; since they ask people they already know, these groups also remain Japanese American in composition.

Because membership in many organizations is by invitation or entry as a group, it is often important that connections begin to be established at an early age. Belonging to one Japanese American organization (through invitation from a friend of relative already in the group) leads to further contacts. From the contacts made in this first organizational affiliation, possibilities open up of joining other Japanese American organizations. For example, in the YMCA Indian Guides, a boys' softball team in the peewee division of *Sansei* League was organized. Without these connections it is difficult to enter into many of the more popular ethnic organizations found in Japanese American communities.

Competition

A related subject is competitiveness. One sign that the high ethnics have been able to separate their personal lives from the nonJapanese American community is that while they are extremely competitive within the Japanese American community, they are relatively noncompetitive in the larger society. They tend to remove themselves entirely from competing in nonJapanese American situations. For example, in Gardena there are beauty contests that only Japanese Americans take part in, such as Miss *Nisei* Week or Miss *Sansei*, and there are beauty contests that the rest of the city, except for the Japanese Americans, compete in. If they do compete against nonJapanese Americans, high ethnics care less about the results. As one high ethnic informant put it - while he likes to win he doesn't feel too badly if he loses in a nonJapanese American competition. But he cares very much if he loses a Japanese American competition. The opinion of the outside society is of little consequence to these high ethnics, for their attention is mainly focused inward.

Within the Japanese American community, the competition can become bitter. Coaches and teams are accused of raiding other teams for their best players. Nonleague games open to any Japanese American are set up, supposedly for the sheer enjoyment of competition. In actuality, they give coaches from the various leagues an opportunity to examine playing abilities and to recruit the outstanding players for their own leagues.

As one means of helping foster father-son closeness, boxwood derby and kite-making contests are held in the Japanese American tribes of Indian Guides. Supposedly fathers and sons work on projects together, but the resultant model racing cars and kites are so elaborate that they obviously required days of labor, without the help of the five and six-year old sons. Rather than encouraging father-son closeness, these contests pit father against father. In addition members of the established cliques will not help new members but, instead, plot among themselves to win all the prizes.

RECIPROCAL OBLIGATION - JAPANESE AMERICAN GIFT GIVING

In addition to friendship networks and organizational participation there is a third and very important means by which ethnicity is maintained, even into the third- and fourth-generations. This is the previously mentioned system of reciprocal obligation in which aid, favors and gifts are expected to be reciprocated. This system stems directly out of the gift-giving practices of Japan, in which traditionally there were complex rules defining who gives to whom, on what occasions, the appropriate gift for each occasion and the way in which the gifts are presented (Befu 1974:208). Although the Japanese American system is just as binding, the specific rules appear to differ.

Johnson (1974) found this system in effect in her work with the Japanese American population in Hawaii. She made an analytical distinction here between two types of reciprocity - generalized and balanced. Generalized reciprocity occurs within the extended family and in friendship circles. The gift exchange is geared to the participants' means and needs and is accompanied by a high degree of sociability. Because the obligation is generally unspecified, the system of exchange creates a diffuse but permanent indebtedness. Balanced reciprocity, which Johnson labels the "*kosai*", can occur across an extremely wide range of people. An exact equivalence of return (generally money) is expected and is time-bound to specified occasions (1974:276-297). This same system, with some modifications, also exists among the Japanese Americans of California.

To a Japanese American, the receipt of any gift or service that is non-economic in nature (i.e, where they are not specifically contracted and paid for) incurs some degree of obligation. High ethnics in particular are very conscious of the obligations incurred and of the need to discharge this obligation at some time in the future. This sense of reciprocity runs through all relationships between Japanese Americans, from the extended family and friends to mere acquaintances. The occasions on which obligation is incurred and the degree of the obligation, however, differ according to the closeness of the social relationship.

Generalized Reciprocity

There is far more exchange of a wider range of goods and services and under more informal conditions between family and friends than between acquaintances. Friends and family will share extra food they might have, do favors for each other when needed, help out in the event of crisis, such as serious illness or financial difficulty and participate in all the ceremonial events of the life cycle starting with birth, through graduation, marriage, and death. No immediate return is expected, for this is a continuing relationship, but sooner or later reciprocity is expected. For most occasions there is no exact reckoning of the amount needed to be returned, rather a far more easy-going expectation that things will eventually balance out.

In some more extreme circumstances, there is a realization that probably no comparable reciprocity can be made. For example, a middle-aged Japanese American doctor with a family was suddenly stricken with a serious heart attack. He was hospitalized for some time and then had a long period of recuperation at home. The family's Japanese American friends quickly mobilized to help care for the children and the house while the wife was occupied with her hospitalized husband. His practice was kept going during his months of recovery by his Japanese American doctor friends who filled in one day a week at his office on their days off. After he was well enough to return to his practice, he and his wife gave their friends expensive gifts and took them out to dinner. These were literally tokens of appreciation. In no way were they seen as discharging his obligation. At the same time, it was realized by all parties that he would probably never have the opportunity to return the favors his friends had done for him.

In any sort of exchange between Japanese Americans, care is taken when offering a gift to at least minimize the surface appearance of the debt. Gifts are often presented in a very casual way - "We can't possibly eat all these strawberries my mother-in-law brought over, so we thought you might like some." In this way the giver implies that the receiver is doing the giver a favor even though both people know that sometime later the receiver will be over with some "extra" cookies she made. Or, an individual might say, "Think nothing about it. It was no trouble at all, and besides I enjoy tinkering with engines" after he has spent a day fixing his friend's car.

There are, however, some areas of exchange between relatives and friends in which the reciprocity becomes less generalized. At birthdays and Christmas, the gifts are carefully calculated to be of about equivalent monetary values. If, for some reason, reciprocity is impossible, prior arrangements must be made beforehand. When one family found itself in financial difficulties, the wife telephoned relatives and friends with whom the family was in an exchange relationship and arranged with them not to exchange gifts that year. If the family had not made this agreement, they would have felt obligated to reciprocate even when they could not have afforded it. There are also times when gifts are given in which a similar reciprocation is expected on the appropriate occasion - the birth of a child, particularly the first born, graduation from high school and college (here gifts, usually monetary, are generally only given from the older generations to the younger generations), weddings, and sometimes before an individual leaves for a long voyage to perhaps Europe or the Orient.

Balanced Reciprocity

Weddings and funerals are the two major events when reciprocity is extended far beyond one's circle of relatives and friends. The reciprocity is of the balanced type. Japanese American weddings tend to be very large - 250-400 guests are normal. Not only are all one's relatives and family and personal friends invited, but also people that one is normally not in a generalized reciprocal relationship with but knows well enough to be in a ceremonial balanced reciprocal relationship, such as parents' business friends, family physician, and old school friends. Japanese American weddings also tend to be expensive, because a formal meal is expected and sometimes there is an open bar. Hors d'oeuvres, cake and punch receptions are seen as a caucasian practice and looked down open.

As in nonJapanese American weddings, records are kept of all the gifts received so the bride can respond with appropriate thank you notes. However, this record is also used as a reference for exact reciprocation in future weddings. Guests calculate the value of their gifts based on the closeness of their ties to the couple or their families, on their own social position and on the type of gift previously given to them by the families in question. The gifts, especially since they are usually not money, are the newlywed couple's property and are not used to pay for the reception or to help the bride's and groom's parents finance their future obligations.

While the large formal reception is for all guests, there is often an additional celebration following the reception limited to relatives and good friends - the people with whom the bride and groom have a continuing generalized reciprocal relationship. These guests have received a verbal invitation - contrasting with the formal invitation to the wedding and reception. The distinction between the formal balanced reciprocal and the informal generalized reciprocal relationships is further marked by the bride's changing from her formal wedding attire, usually western style gown and veil, to a more casual dress. Food and drinks are served and the wedding gifts are ceremonially unwrapped and displayed to all the guests[2]. This post-reception ceremony in no way relieves the bride and groom and their families of their obligations to reciprocate in a similar fashion at future weddings. Rather, it is a reaffirmation of the closer, more sociable and more enduring generalized reciprocal relationships they hold with these selected guests.

Funerals include the widest possible range of people from the closest of family and friends to the remotest of acquaintances. It is here that the strictest and most exacting reckoning of reciprocal obligation occurs. Originally coming from the Japanese Buddhist practice of contributing small sums of money to help the bereaved family pay for the necessary incense and other funeral expenses, a monetary contribution known as *koden* continues to be given at almost all Japanese American funerals - Buddhist and Christian. Except for the close family, everyone who knew the deceased or his family gives *koden*, whether they attend the funeral service or not. This in turn obligates the family of the deceased to reciprocate in exact amounts to all donors and their families.

In each family, when *koden* is given, a careful record is made of the amount and the name of the giver. This *koden* book is then kept in the care of the family head, and copies are distributed to each of his children (as new family heads) so that they know to who and how much *koden* to reciprocate.

The system of *koden* may be thought of as an ever widening circle, particularly for the oldest son of each family. As the representative of his family he must reciprocate *koden* given at his parents' funerals by his friends, his parents' friends and his co-workers and neighbors. This reciprocation extends not just to the person who gave *koden*, but also to any member of their family. This return payment of *koden* does not actually cancel one's obligations, but simply continues on to an ever-expanding group of people.

Giving *koden* is an expensive proposition, particularly as with increasing age one incurs increasing obligations. It used to be a matter of a few dollars but now the standard minimum amount is $10 if the deceased is not known to the giver at all, $15 if the deceased is known to the giver but not well, and increasing amounts depending upon the closeness of the relationship. It is not unusual for amounts between $50-$100 to be given, and close friends may send both funeral wreathes and *koden*.

The children of the family of the deceased do not give *koden* but have flower arrangements made with ribbons saying "Beloved Grandmother" or "Beloved Uncle". These arrangements are standard western style arrangements or in the shape of objects representing interests of the deceased, such as a bowling ball and pins if he liked to bowl, and are placed near the casket. Wreathes from close friends and organizations the deceased was a member of are placed along the sides of the sanctuary where the service takes place. The family of the deceased sends a thank you acknowledgement to each giver, along with a token gift. This used to be a box of coffee candy or Japanese rice crackers, but now either a book of stamps is sent or a donation is given to a charity, church or school and is so stated on the thank you note. Again, this does not relieve or lessen the obligation to reciprocate.

Usually enough *koden* is collected to pay for the funeral and all related expenses which, whether Buddhist or Christian, include such items as printing of thank you notes, thank you gifts, printing of the funeral program, and feeding people, often at a restaurant after the burial service, as well as the usual funeral expenses of flowers, casket, funeral director's services, minister's or priest's services and the like. Buddhist funerals tend to be more expensive since there are more services and more which require the service of a priest or priests. On the day of death a service is held for family and close friends, the funeral service requires a number of priests, particularly since the service is usually conducted in Japanese and English, a burial service occurs the following day attended by family and friends, a seven day service is held for family and close friends, and a series of memorial services are held at various yearly intervals.

Although in some ways burdensome, most *sansei* appear to feel that *koden* is very useful. No family is suddenly faced with a large funeral bill, for through the giving of *koden*, they have, in a way, been paying for it in small increments over a period of years. They do not see *koden* as wasted money, for when it is their time they will get it back. In addition, they feel that it is a concrete way of showing that they care, and in a more practical manner than with flowers.

While the funeral service and giving of *koden* draw upon the widest circle of family, friends and acquaintances in a balanced reciprocal relationship, there are also formal and informal ceremonies surrounding the deceased and his family which draw upon smaller circles of kin and friends who are in a more generalized reciprocal relationship. Shortly after a death, relatives and friends visit at the home of the deceased or the nearest relative to offer their sympathies, bring gifts of food and to help out in any way necessary. They attend the funeral service, the burial service and the funeral meals given by the deceased's family following both services. If the services are Buddhist, relatives and close friends also attend the memorial services and as bring gifts of food for the meal that follows each service. The first-generation immigrants also bring *koden* to the memorial services to help defray expenses, but the younger generations do not.

Functions of Reciprocal Obligation

The custom of institutionalized gift-giving was brought to America by the *issei*, the immigrant generation. No doubt it served as an important means of insurance for these struggling people, particularly in times of crisis and in meeting family funeral expenses.

Today most families are financially secure enough that they can afford to meet their own expenses. Yet reciprocity continues to flourish, even among the later generations who do not always totally understand the more formal aspects of reciprocity, e.g. funerals and *koden* and must turn to their parents for guidance. This is in part due to the fact that, burdensome as it is at times, it is impossible to drop out of this system, particularly *koden*, without totally dropping out of participation in the ethnic community. Reciprocal obligation is a value deeply instilled into each individual from childhood[3], and the social pressures to conform to this practice are considerable. To be a pariah among Japanese Americans, all a Japanese American needs to do is not give *koden*.

Reciprocal obligation also plays an important function in helping to maintain ethnicity. It helps to foster a sense of community. It puts an individual into at least a symbolic relationship with a very wide range of Japanese Americans. It intensifies the social and personal relationships found between kin and friends through a continual and diffuse exchange of goods and services. Additionally, since this elaborate system is a Japanese and Japanese American one, only people of Japanese ancestry participate in it; nonJapanese Americans are partitioned off from an important aspect of Japanese American personal and community life.

SUMMARY

In an area in which Japanese Americans are clustered to form a geographic community, ethnicity is established and maintained in the later generations in a number of ways. The Japanese American system of friendship formation and friendship cliques intensify and extend relationships between Japanese Americans while limiting social interactions with nonJapanese Americans.

Only after friendship networks are established does an individual enter ethnic organizations, and then usually only as part of an already established group or to join friends who are in the organization. Consequently, while organizational membership can help to extend social networks, it primarily serves to intensify previously existing relationships. If this is successful, acquaintances become friends, and casual friends become good friends. These relationships are then expanded outside of the institutional setting. (This sequence is the reverse of what occurs in the suburban nonJapanese American areas of Orange county and will be discussed in the following chapter.) Also, because institutions and organizations both overtly and covertly exclude nonJapanese Americans, this all occurs in the comfortable confines of a Japanese American environment.

Finally, the system of reciprocal obligation promotes cohesion with the ethnic community. On its formal level, it operates to put a wide range of Japanese Americans in symbolic contact with each other. On its more informal level, it serves to intensify relations with kin and friends in an enduring exchange of gifts and services, perpetuating their relationships.

ETHNICITY IN THE SUBURBS

It is often assumed that ethnicity flourishes only in the lower socioeconomic, ethnically homogeneous neighborhood, and as upward social and economic mobility moves individuals into the middle and upper-middle class suburbs, they lose their ethnicity (e.g. Kagiwada 1969; Levine and Montero 1973). Two reasons are frequently cited for this loss: 1) integration into white neighborhood networks is desired and 2) even if interaction with members of their own ethnic category is desired, opportunities for such in the nonethnic (in the sense of residential concentration) suburbs are limited, at best.

Japanese Americans in Gardena are aware of this problem. Consequently, those for whom their ethnicity is highly significant feel that it would be very difficult to move out of the city, even though they are concerned about the growing number of black residents. Because Los Angeles county has a longer history of development than Orange county, available housing tends to be scarcer, smaller, older and more expensive than for a comparable dwelling in Orange county. Even so, if they feel the need to relocate, they prefer to move to the adjoining city of Torrance. Housing is still older and more expensive, but this city is not yet undergoing the racial flux that Gardena is experiencing. Torrance is perceived by Japanese Americans to be a higher income, and therefore more desirable area. It is so near to Gardena that even though it is a predominantly white area, they can easily maintain their existing ethnic networks and memberships in Japanese American organizations.

A look at middle and upper-middle class Japanese Americans in Orange county, however, reveals that a loss of ethnicity need not occur. Obviously, it is easy for them to assimilate through inertia, since they work and live with mostly nonJapanese Americans and their children may be only one of a small number of Asians in their schools. To become or remain ethnic involves some amount of effort. Commuting on a regular basis to Gardena or other areas of Japanese American concentration is usually too difficult. Despite these difficulties, ethnicity can and does flourish in the upper-middle class suburbs of Orange county.

DESIRE FOR ETHNICITY

Although there was a slight correlation between income and ethnicity in that there was a tendency for individuals with higher incomes to have lower ethnic scores, the relationship was not strong enough to be significant. Certainly both the high and low ethnics interviewed in Orange county had more interaction and formed more friendships with nonJapanese Americans than did the high and low ethnics interviewed in Gardena. The Orange County Japanese Americans felt comfortable in dealing with either Japanese Americans or caucasians, had moved to Orange county for the economic advantages a newly developing community offered, and preferred living in a more affluent neighborhood, even though they might be the only Japanese American family in the area. In behavior and appearance they fit easily into their upper-middle class milieu. The women, in particular, are often fashionably dressed and coiffed, highly educated and articulate, knowledgeable in etiquette and gracious as hostesses.

Yet despite their ease in dealing with either community, these high ethnics prefer to socialize with other Japanese Americans and they seek out and make opportunities to do so. While they socialize with and have friends who are not Japanese American, their closest friends are usually Japanese American. As one woman stated, she divides her friends into two groups - her "social friends" who are nonJapanese American and her "social and crisis friends" (those who will come to her aid) who are Japanese American. They turn to Japanese Americans for their closest, most meaningful relationships because they feel they have learned from experience that Japanese Americans are far more sincere and committed in their friendships. NonJapanese Americans cannot be depended on in times of trouble. Even though the Japanese Americans of this socioeconomic background know the ways of the larger society, they find that they still differ in a number of subtle but significant ways.

INSTITUTIONAL METHODS FOR MAINTAINING ETHNICITY

Given the geographic residential scattering of the Orange county Japanese American, how can ethnic networks be established for those who desire them? Within the cities of Los Angeles county that have heavily concentrated ethnic enclaves, relationships between Japanese Americans occur informally, naturally and frequently, and friendships form without the need for formal institutional structures. In the suburbs, however, Japanese Americans usually need to turn to Japanese American institutions in order to make contact with other Japanese Americans. It is through these formal organizations that they begin to establish informal relationships. The absence of residential clustering requires that the ethnic organizations draw from a fairly large geographic area rather than from a single neighborhood or even a single city. There is a Japanese American community in Orange County, but it is far more fragmented and less territorial in nature.

There appear to be three basic types of institutions in Orange county which serve to establish and maintain ethnic ties. One of them has existed in the Orange county Japanese American community for a number of years and is a fairly traditional means of maintaining ethnicity. The other two are somewhat more recent developments.

The Ethnic Church

For many American ethnic groups, the ethnic church has served far more than its obvious religious functions. For the Irish Americans, the Greek Americans, the Italian Americans, the American Jews and for others the religious institution has been an important vehicle for bringing fellow ethnics together, for focusing and intensifying their ethnic identification. It sponsors and provides the facilities for the activities that serve to establish and increase ethnic networks among its members.

This is also the case with the Japanese Americans. Unlike many other ethnic groups, however, their identification with a particular religion is not an intrinsic part of their ethnic identity, as is the case with Catholicism and Italian Americans, Judaism and American Jews, and Greek Orthodoxy and Greek Americans. There are two major religions observed in the Japanese American population–Buddhism and Christianity. Whether Buddhist or Christian, however, if the congregation is primarily Japanese American in composition, the church serves as an important facilitator of ethnicity. The church is particularly important where the Japanese Americans are geographically scattered as in Orange county.

Many Japanese Americans attend an ethnic church for more than religious purposes. According to Japanese American norms, it is far more acceptable to talk with a Japanese American with whom one is unacquainted when they both belong to the same organization. Conversely, it is far less acceptable to attempt a conversation with an unknown Japanese American passing by on the street or in the market. The church provides its members with opportunities they might not otherwise have to permissibly meet and socialize with Japanese Americans. Church activities are also an important means by which the children who attend schools in which there are very few Japanese Americans can socialize with Japanese American children of the same and, importantly, the opposite sex.

Brookside Christian Church

There are a number of Japanese American churches in Orange county - both Christian and Buddhist - among which is Brookside Christian Church. Supposedly it was the first Japanese mission in Orange county and was formed in 1904 on a corner of a Japanese owned flower farm. It was very small and the congregation consisted of Orange county Japanese farming families, a number of whom have become quite wealthy. Their only opportunity to socialize with other Japanese American families was during the weekends. The church served as a focus for the social life of these Japanese American farmers who lived in predominantly nonJapanese American areas.

From its small facilities on a Japanese American farm the church eventually moved to an area of Orange county that is mainly lower income and nonJapanese American in composition. As a result, the members of the congregation continue to come from communities all over Orange county. In the 1950s and 1960s the church was nearly moribund as its congregation shrunk. With a younger, more active leadership and the growing number of young Japanese American families who are moving into Orange county, however, the church is flourishing and once again in need of larger facilities.

There is, however, a split in the church between the old founding families and the newer group now in power. The individuals making up the newer group are seen as usurpers.

Although they continue to support the church financially out of a sense of loyalty, a group made up of the founding families has basically removed itself from any participation in the church. They deplore the path they see their church taking, for the present group in power is highly religious and very fundamentalist in tone. To the original group, this is contrary to their sect of Christianity. They see the other group as too religious and too disorganized in church matters, while the other side sees them as insufficiently religious and too businesslike in church matters.

The present congregation is predominantly American-born, but the church also has a very tiny foreign-born congregation, like nearly every Japanese American church whether Christian or Buddhist. There are two ministers - a second-generation Japanese American for the English service and a Japanese national for the Japanese service. Efforts are made to integrate the Japanese congregation into many of the activities of the American congregation but generally, due to language and cultural differences, they remain separate.

Brookside Church: Ethnicity in a Nonethnic Community

In the American congregation there are two basic types of church goers - the social ethnic members and the ethnic Born Again Christians. Social ethnic members attend this church primarily so that they, and particularly their children, have an opportunity to interact with other Japanese Americans. Rather than attend their neighborhood Christian church whose congregation and minister are caucasian, they drive the 20-30 miles to attend Brookside. Those who are more religiously inclined may feel their neighborhood church provides a better religious education. Some of these parents attend religious services only sporadically and either wait in their cars in the church parking lot (fathers in particular) while their children attend Sunday school or drop them off and then return to pick them up after services are over. Although not attending services regularly, they help out at and attend many of the nonreligious activities of the church. This serves to acquaint them with other Japanese Americans. Furthermore, as their children form friendships with other children in the church, and occasionally wish to socialize outside of the church setting, parents need to serve as chauffeurs. This again puts them in contact with other Japanese American families. Finally, due to the numerous activities of the church, particularly family oriented ones, many of the noninvolved ethnic members become more and more involved. From chauffeurs they become participants, and eventually some of them join the Born Again Christian group (this process will be discussed in detail below).

In addition to the various Sunday religious activities which run from 9:30 to noon, Brookside sponsors a large number of weekly and monthly religious and nonreligious activities. Every Friday evening there is Family Night, which is both social and religious in nature. On Wednesdays there are bible study groups, and there is a Japanese language class one evening a week. There are also church picnics, beach parties, potluck dinners, skating parties, camping trips, square dances and the like, all of which give both the religious and nonreligious members a chance to socialize and become friends with each other. The church also sponsors a number of boys and girls basketball and softball teams which belong to a Japanese American athletic league in Orange county. There are many activities geared specifically for the adolescents - dances, parties, athletic competitions, etc.

The church has four major fund raising events each year - two rummage sales, an International Food Festival in the fall and a Hawaiian Night in the early summer. The International Food Festival is basically a carnival with Japanese, Chinese and Mexican food, games of skill and chance, and sales of plants, vegetables and handmade gift items. The Hawaiian Night is a Japanese American version of a Hawaiian banquet or luau along with Hawaiian dancing. Both of these affairs involve tremendous amounts of planning, work and manpower on the part of the congregation. This is partly due to the size and elaborateness of these two undertakings - booths and stages need to be built, a wide variety of food and gift items need to be prepared, etc.

The nature of the food served at Japanese American events, however, puts on additional demands. To a Japanese American a carnival does not mean only hot dogs, hamburgers and cotton candy (all foods that are fairly simple to prepare); it means *sushi* (rolls of vinegared rice filled with strips of cooked and seasoned vegetables and wrapped in dried sheets of seaweed), *teriyaki* beef (thinly sliced - 1/16th of an inch - strips of beef which are threaded on bamboo skewers, marinated in a sauce and charcoal broiled), *wonton* (little deep fried meat-filled dumplings), *chow mein* (boiled and pan fried noodles topped with a stir-fried mixture of chopped meat and vegetables in a sauce), *tempura* (shrimp and sliced vegetables dipped in a special batter and deep fried) and *manju* (little pastries filled with a sweetened bean paste), in addition to Mexican food and the traditional hot dogs and hamburgers. The Hawaiian Night dinner is as elaborate, consisting of a plate of steamed rice, *teriyaki* beef strips, quasi-Hawaiian style roast pork, *chow mein*, a guava gelatin, a fruit kebab, *lomi lomi* salmon (a mixture of salted salmon, tomatoes and onions), *poi* (a paste of pounded taro root), and Japanese-style pickled cabbage. All of these foods require days of preparation and many people to help both before and during the event. Consequently, these events not only serve as fund-raisers but also serve to intensify relationships within the church.

The structure of the ethnic church and the many activities it sponsors may be little different from those of any other active mainstream society church. What is significant for the maintenance of ethnicity in a nonethnic community is that it all takes place in an institutionally formed ethnic environment. The only Japanese American family on the block can, through participation in a Japanese American church, choose to worship and socialize mainly with Japanese Americans.

This raises an important question - how is a Japanese American church kept Japanese American? Theoretically a Christian church is open to everyone, regardless of ethnic category. It would seem to be particularly difficult to maintain the "ethnic purity" of the congregation when it is located in a nonJapanese American area and follows a mainstream religion. Despite this apparent problem, Brookside as well as most other Japanese American Christian churches have managed to successfully discourage nonJapanese Americans from joining. This is not done deliberately nor even consciously. First, most caucasians, not being used to being in a minority position, probably do not want to attend a Japanese American church on their own, regardless of convenience. There are a few caucasian members at Brookside, but the majority of them have a Japanese American connection - they are married to Japanese American members. There are occasional caucasian visitors and they are always greeted with cordiality by a few of the church officials. But the majority of the congregation, being less out-going in nature with strangers, tend to politely ignore the newcomer. The caucasian, unless he is particularly anxious to be with Japanese Americans, will leave feeling that the church is in some way not very "warm." There are a very small number of caucasians (about six) without any Japanese American connection who regularly attend services. One couple has served in churches in Japan and Hawaii so they are very familiar with Japanese American ways and, as a result, are well accepted into the church. The others appear to be a familiar type to Japanese

Americans - misfits in their own mainstream society who are attracted to another culture. Even though these few are fairly regular in attendance and even take part in church activities, they still continue to be set apart by the rest of the congregation. The pews they sit in are the last to be filled and will only be filled if there is nowhere else for the Japanese Americans to sit. People are less likely to spontaneously interact with them after services are over and they do not appear to be part of any of the closer, informal networks that emerged from the church. In fact, after several months one couple no longer attended and the rest attend services only sporadically.

If, for some reason, a Japanese American church is unable to maintain its ethnic distinctiveness due to the influx of white members, what usually occurs is that rather than integrate, the original Japanese American members leave and no more enter to take their places. According to an informant, this is what is happening to one such church in Los Angeles. Even in areas of Los Angeles of formerly heavy Japanese American concentration, the neighborhood Japanese American church remains ethnic in composition despite the shift in the area's ethnic composition. It's members, remaining loyal to their church, continue to commute from their new area of residence. Hence, a number of Japanese American churches survive even though the neighborhood they remain in has become predominantly black or Hispanic.

Brookside Church: Born Again Christians and Ethnicity

In addition to its social ethnic church goers, Brookside has a large core of ethnic Born Again Christians. Many of the members of this group are the leaders of the church. For this group, the more religious they become, philosophically the less ethnic they become, as their identities as Christians become of more significance in their lives than their identities as Japanese Americans. Yet, the more religious they become the more their social and religious networks and activities are conducted solely with other Japanese Americans. They become more involved in church activities and their family lives begin to revolve around the church - a Japanese American church with a Japanese American congregation and a Japanese American minister. They try to be practicing Christians, but they practice their religion mainly among other Japanese Americans. They claim that their religious commitment takes primacy over ethnic concerns. They would prefer that their children marry a Christian nonJapanese American than a nonChristian Japanese American, although they hope for a Christian Japanese American. Along with an increased involvement with Japanese Americans due to the numerous church activities they take part in, they also have a deeper involvement with fellow Born Again Christian Japanese Americans. Along with ethnic ties, they now share a religious tie. And as they become more involved in church related events, they have less time for their nonJapanese American friends.

Springing from the church are a number of different organizations and activities which serve to link a geographically wider and wider network of Japanese American Christians. This culminates once a year with a week long religious retreat, arranged by the Japanese Evangelical Missionary Society, at a religious camp called Mt. Hermon in northern California. Although drawing Japanese American Christians mainly from California, a number of people also come from ethnic churches in Washington and Utah. At the time this research was conducted this annual retreat had been occurring for 29 years. It had grown from a small group in its initial years to such a size that the main campsite could no longer accommodate everyone. Instead adults and young children were at the main camp while the junior high schoolers, the senior high schoolers and the collegians and young adults each had their own camps, with their own religious and social activities. There were approximately 600-700 people at the main camp with smaller numbers at the various children's camps - in all approximately 1500 people.

At this camp in the woods of northern California, except for a few caucasian spouses, the camp employees and the key speaker, there were nothing but Japanese American Christians. As well as providing numerous opportunities to get to know other Japanese Americans, the retreat also served to intensify still further the ethnic-religious relationships formed at Brookside, for they lived, ate, socialized and worshipped together for a week without the intrusion of the outside society. In addition to participating in all the formal activities of the retreat, the group from Brookside, coming prepared with a supply of food, frequently withdrew during the break in the morning service to socialize and snack with each other in one of their rooms. After the evening service, they had parties at a member's cabin. Although they often invited nonBrookside friends as well, the majority of the people were from Brookside. These occasions, as well as providing further opportunities for socializing, also served as opportunities to share emotional religious feelings with each other. Sharing and crying together contributed to the intensification of identifying with Brookside which would thereby decrease the chances that these Christians would wish to seek Christianity in another church, much less a nonJapanese American church.

Particularly for the adolescents, relationships formed in camp were often maintained through correspondence during the year. Since many families return yearly to Mt. Hermon, these relationships are renewed at each retreat. In this way an individual establishes and extends his ethnic network. This is particularly important for Japanese Americans because they find it difficult to interact with another Japanese American unless they have been introduced by a common acquaintance (Hosokawa 1973:214) or at least have a common friend.

Brookside Church: Becoming a Born Again Japanese American Christian

Many of the present Born Again Christians have come from the ranks of the social ethnic church goers, some of whom have even been initially hostile to the religious elements of Brookside. The process of their conversion to a more religious Christianity and, thereby, their further involvement with Japanese Americans, has many variations, but a somewhat typical case follows.

The Okayama family was the only Japanese American family in their upper-middle class predominantly white Orange county neighborhood they lived in. In school their children were the only Japanese Americans in their grade levels. Consequently, all their playmates were white. Hearing of Brookside from a Japanese American friend who lived in Los Angeles and wanting their children to know other Japanese Americans, the parents decided to send them to Sunday School. They themselves, however, rarely attended because it was boring to sit through the sermon. They felt they didn't need religion since they had gone to church as children. Their children, after a short period of strangeness because they had never been with so many Japanese Americans before, enjoyed the Sunday School activities, began to make friends, and wanted to come to some of the other activities their fellow students told them about. The mother found herself chauffeuring the children to and from the church more often and because she was there more often and was frequently invited to attend various activities, she began to know some of the women in the church. Meanwhile her children began to ask why she and their father rarely came to church, especially since family togetherness was stressed so much at Brookside. Partly out of feelings of guilt, and partly because she now knew a few of the members and so felt more comfortable, the mother began to attend fairly regularly. The father slept late on Sundays, although he sometimes attended some of the social activities of the church, particularly because many of them were family oriented; he began to know some of the men in the congregation.

Meanwhile, the time for Mt. Hermon was coming up. Children who had previously attended told glowing tales of their experiences and urged the Okayama children to come with them for that year's retreat. The children, enthused by their friends' reports, begged their parents to have the family attend. After some discussion with friends who also spoke enthusiastically about it, Mrs. Okayama decided to let her children go. She also decided to attend herself, partly out of curiosity, partly out of a growing desire for some religious commitment and partly out of the urging of her children and friends. Mr. Okayama, dismayed by what he saw as the growing religiosity of his family, refused to go because he didn't want to be around so many Christians for an entire week and also, had to work.

Mrs. Okayama and her children went. In that isolated religious environment, as some of their friends stepped forward in the light of the evening campfire and either made a commitment or renewed a former commitment to Jesus and Christianity, the children were also inspired to make a commitment. Mrs. Okayama did not, although she was moved by some of the testimony given by people in the adult camp on how Christianity had changed their lives.

During the following year, efforts were made by Brookside to maintain the commitments given by their members at Mt. Hermon through church retreats and other activities. These served to revive some of the emotional peaks felt by these people. Mrs. Okayama and her children became even more involved in church activities, and she made a number of close friends with whom she and her husband socialized outside of the church as well. The next year Mr. Okayama came reluctantly to Mt. Hermon, under the urging of his family and other members of the church (although knowing his religious apathy they were careful to stress the social aspects of the retreat). There Mrs. Okayama made her commitment. Mr. Okayama did not.

The religious conversion of Mrs. Okayama caused some problems between her and her nonreligious husband. However, her friends at Brookside counseled patience and, with family life centering even more around church sponsored activities and church friends, Mr. Okayama was put even more into a Japanese American and a Christian environment. His wife conscientiously attempted to change and improve herself and, noticing and being impressed by his wife's actions, he began quietly to become more accepting of religion. This process took a number of years. Finally, three years after the conversion of his wife, Mr. Okayama, by now a social ethnic. surprised his family and friends by publicly committing his life to Christ at Mr. Hermon. He thus joined the ranks of the Born Again Japanese American Christians.

The Ethnic Athletic Leagues

A second institutional means by which Japanese Americans have an opportunity to meet and become friends are the Japanese American children's athletic organizations, such as the Southeast Youth Organization and the Japanese Optimist's League. The Southeast Youth Organization (SEYO) was initially formed in 1964 by members of the Japanese American community of Orange county. By limiting membership to children of Japanese ancestry, its overt purpose is to provide the often times physically smaller Japanese American children with opportunities to compete successfully in athletic events. More importantly, however, participation in this athletic organization serves to increase the interactions of Japanese Americans with each other, both for the children themselves who are the players and for their parents who are the coaches, officers, spectators and chauffeurs.

Like its counterparts in Los Angeles county, SEYO has various Japanese American service clubs, business organizations and churches sponsor boys and girls basketball and softball teams that compete in age-graded leagues. Since children come into the organization as an already formed and sponsored team, they obviously already know at least a minimum number of Japanese Americans. Participation, therefore, tends to be a secondary rather than a primary means of establishing ethnic ties for the individual. However, SEYO does function to intensify pre-existing ethnic relationships. Team members are drawn from a larger ethnic organization, such as Brookside Christian Church. The children, already knowing each other from church activities, are provided with further opportunities for interaction in a different setting as members of a smaller group. In addition, SEYO acts as an unifier for the extremely dispersed Orange county Japanese American community. Through the sponsoring of teams or donations to the league, diverse Japanese American organizations - religious, service, business, and social - can participate together in an event that is for Japanese Americans. It is a means by which the development of a sense of belonging to a larger community is encouraged.

SEYO not only serves to increase interaction with Japanese Americans but also serves to further limit interaction with the outside nonethnic community of Orange county. By joining a Japanese American athletic club a child has less contact with nonJapanese Americans than he would have had if he had joined a nonethnic athletic club. When it is the basketball or softball season, much of a child's time is taken up with practice or with games which, as a result, limit the amount of time he has to spend with his nonJapanese American neighbors and school friends.

Finally, it may also be speculated that interaction with Japanese Americans reinforces distinctive behavior patterns which result in further discomfort when dealing with the outside society. For example, informants have said that Japanese Americans are less aggressive than whites. In addition to their smaller physiques, as further rationale for the need for a separate Japanese American athletic program, parents state that their children find it difficult competing against the more aggressive white players. However, as was pointed out by a low ethnic of Orange county whose child plays in a caucasian league, by competing only with other less aggressive Japanese Americans they have little chance to learn how to be more aggressive and, thereby, be able to compete in the larger society in general.

The Ethnic Social and Service Clubs

The third way by which upper-middle class Japanese Americans form ethnic networks is through participation in the Japanese American social and service clubs that exist in Orange county. In form and function they mirror clubs found in the mainstream society. Many of them are in fact their exact counterparts, except Japanese American in membership. Rather than belong to the Optimists Club or the VFW post that is in his city of residence, a high ethnic Japanese American prefers to join a Japanese American Optimists Club, or a Japanese American VFW post, even if it is in another city. His reasons for joining the ethnic rather than the mainstream community club are similar to those of his ethnic brethren who live in an ethnic enclave. The reasons vary from having a sense of comfort when dealing with fellow ethnics to being a good means of establishing business contacts. However, as a means of establishing and extending informal relationships with other Japanese Americans, membership in these organizations takes on more importance in this geographically scattered ethnic community than it would in an ethnic enclave.

Large scale ethnic community organizations such as the Japanese American church or the athletic league are open to a wide range of socioeconomic backgrounds (although in Orange county there tends to be less of a range - from middle class small businessmen to upper-middle class professionals and businessmen - than would be found in Los Angeles county). There is a considerable amount of mingling among the levels. However, membership in the social clubs can be limited to a narrower range of social class. This is the case, especially in the women's clubs. Here, not only does a woman meet and ultimately form friendships with other Japanese American women, but the friendships and resultant socializing are with Japanese Americans of the "proper" background - nonJapanese Americans and lower income Japanese Americans are excluded since membership is by invitation only.

The Socialites

There are a number of Japanese American women's social and service clubs in Orange county. Although each such organization differs from the others in various aspects, there are enough similarities that an examination of one particular club can, to a great extent, serve as an examination of all.

The Socialites is a women's club of 65 members. It was begun about 10 years ago when two wives of Orange county doctors felt it would be enjoyable to meet other Asian American women in the area. Since they were fairly new to the area and did not know any others, they culled Oriental names from the local phone book and sent out invitations. Janet, a third-generation Japanese American married to a dentist, received an invitation and decided to attend. Her family had recently moved into Orange county from Los Angeles and did not know many people, much less Orientals. She thought it would be fun and would be a means to start her social life in the area.

Originally the intention had been to meet informally for coffee at one of their homes four times a year rather than to be a formal organization. However, the women who initially participated enjoyed it so much they wanted to meet more often and have more activities, both among themselves and with their families. As a result, The Socialites was formed and has a constitution, by-laws, a president, first and second vice-presidents, recording and corresponding secretaries, a treasurer and a board of directors, in addition to various project or activity chairwomen. There are four business meetings a year, although at least once a month there is some type of meeting of various committees. Annual dues are collected to defray the cost of the club newsletter. The club is basically social in nature. Particularly for newcomers to the county, it can be the basis of their social lives until they begin to establish informal relationships on their own. Three times a year the Socialites has evening social events at which the husbands are present (dinners, parties, etc.). There are also various organized club activities such as trips to art shows, luncheons and smaller group classes in flower arrangement, gourmet cooking and high fashion sewing. The women are also concerned that their children get to know other Oriental children of the upper-middle class, so they try to include children's and family events. They are considering forming another organization for the adolescents in the hopes that their children will socialize with each other on a regular basis.

The club also has various community service projects. One of them is a scholarship fund for Asian American children who are going to attend college as pre-medical, pre-dental or pre-law students, or who want to attend school in any of these professions. In previous years the club had raised money for various charity organizations that helped people regardless of race. This year, although it was not an unanimous decision, club members decided that they should help their own and restricted the fund to Asians. Janet, who had been the fund raising chairwoman for a number of years felt that sentiment to be fair since The Socialites is an Oriental organization. She has found that it is more difficult to raise money, however, since she can no longer ask caucasians for contributions to a cause that only benefits the Orientals.

When it was first organized, invitations were sent blindly to Oriental names found in the telephone book. Now, however, membership is only by invitation, through the sponsorship of an established member. There are also specific criteria for membership- women must be Asian American or the spouse of an Asian American, their husband must belong to a Los Angeles or Orange county medical, dental or legal association, they must reside in Orange county and be English speaking. Wives of credit dentists and foreign professionals are not acceptable, for the women feel the former are economic shysters who are giving the dental profession a bad reputation and the latter are usually poorly trained and would have a language problem in dealing with this American organization. Admittance of the spouses of either type would, as a result, lower the social level of the club.

The Socialites has been an invaluable means by which upper-middle class Asian American wives of doctors, dentists and lawyers in Orange county have been able to meet each other and form close friendships. Many of its members feel that if it were not for this club, they probably would never have met each other. A number of individuals have formed their closest friendships through the club. By participating in the organized club activities, and particularly in the smaller interest groups which facilitate intensive interaction with a smaller number of people with similar interests, women get to know each other and begin to socialize with selected individuals privately as well.

Ironically, because The Socialites has functioned so effectively to establish, increase and intensify ethnic ties, it now faces several problems. Because many of its members are good friends who socialize outside of any club setting, the club presently has difficulty getting people to attend its social functions. Where previously there was a high attendance rate at every event, due to the members' otherwise limited social lives and their desire to interact with people who were possible friends, now there is less impetus. For example, after dining at home with friends one night, there is less need to see them at a Socialites event the next night. Another problem that has emerged is that after years of intensive socializing with each other, the original members have become quite clannish. Therefore, it is difficult for new members to break into and become part of these pre-established communication and interaction networks. Because of this, the club has not been able to provide an effective means for the integration of newcomers. Consequently, there is not at any one time a large enough group of new members and emergent leadership to develop new interaction lines where they are needed and desired but do not already exist. Thus, there is a tendency for new members to be less involved and to eventually drop out. The Socialites now only sponsors a small number of new members every year, partly because they have become more discriminating in their selections and because, according to Janet, there are smaller numbers of Asian American professional families moving into the area; the various communities of Orange county are no longer growing as rapidly and are reaching the maximum level of professionals that they can utilize effectively.

It is also interesting to note that even though The Socialites consists of both Japanese and Chinese Americans, it has not resulted in much inter-ethnic mixing outside of club activities. Japanese Americans prefer to socialize with their Japanese American friends and the same holds true for the Chinese Americans. In addition, some feelings of resentment are emerging because a number of the Japanese American members feel they do far more work for the club than do most of the Chinese American members. Furthermore, it was recently noticed and commented on that for a Chinese gourmet dinner arranged by the club, both Chinese and Japanese Americans attended whereas for a later Japanese gourmet dinner only the Japanese Americans showed up. This perception of Chinese American and Japanese American differences could possibly become a serious source of internal conflict since reciprocity is a very important trait among Japanese Americans.

SUMMARY AND CONCLUSION

Japanese Americans in Orange county are widely dispersed geographically. They live and interact mainly in a nonJapanese American environment, not infrequently being the only Asian family or one of only a few families in the area. Not only are there frequent opportunities to integrate totally into the mainstream society, but their abilities to do so are very high. Many are highly educated, are in well paying prestigious professions, encounter little if any discrimination on the part of nonJapanese Americans, are for all purposes totally acculturated since they are now the third and fourth generations in America and, being accustomed to living mainly with caucasians of the same high socioeconomic level, are used to, comfortable in, and able to deal with the dominant community. When contrasted to many of the Japanese American housewives in Gardena, who reside in areas of the city where much of their neighborhood is composed of other Japanese American families, Orange county women often have more nonJapanese American friends and socialize more often with them.

In accord with earlier research on ethnicity, given this situation, ethnicity should be dying out in the middle and upper-middle class suburbs of Orange county. In reality, ethnicity survives and flourishes for many Japanese Americans in these suburbs.

The ethnicity displayed here is not of the so-called "returning to one's roots" variety. Many have not been to Japan, have no overwhelming desire to do so, and few interact much with or feel very comfortable with the Japanese nationals residing in the area. They are also not part of the move towards a somewhat more politically viable pan-Asian American identity that the politically radical and activist Japanese Americans of Los Angeles are attempting to establish. (Some asked "What's an Asian American? Is it a Japanese American?") The ethnicity to be found here is of a far more subtle but more deeply rooted and more natural sort. These middle class and upper-middle class Japanese Americans want to be with each other because they find comfort in doing so. They still share, or feel they share, a number of values, attitudes and behaviors with each other that distinguish themselves as Japanese Americans from the outside society. While integrating members of the outside community into certain spheres of their lives, they reserve much of the more meaningful parts of their lives for the Japanese American community. They have both white and Japanese American friends, but their Japanese American friends are the more intimate and the ones to whom they automatically turn in times of trouble. Whites can be friends, but Japanese Americans are part of an individual's ethnic "extended family."

While these suburbanites share with the Los Angeles Japanese Americans the desire to be with "their own kind," they necessarily differ in the ways in which their ethnic networks can be established and extended. Having far less of an opportunity, at least initially, to meet and interact informally with their fellow ethnics without institutional mediation, they must seek their potential friends through participation in formal organizations. These organizations not only serve to bring Japanese Americans in, but keep the pervasive white community out, thereby maintaining the ethnic environment desired by its members. Three major ethnic institutions in Orange county - the Japanese American Buddhist and Christian churches, the Japanese American athletic leagues and the Japanese American social and service clubs - function effectively to provide a structured, protected and acceptable setting in which to establish the more personally satisfying informal ethnic relationships. In addition, because membership in these institutions often crosscut, complement and reinforce each other, Japanese Americans successfully extend and intensify their ethnic networks. Ultimately, although they live in an overwhelmingly white world, much of their personal lives are carried out in an exclusively Japanese American one.

BECOMING LOW ETHNIC, BECOMING HIGH ETHNIC

The focus of this study has been on the nature of ethnicity among later generations. Given that ethnicity is not inborn, the questions arise: how and why does a person become ethnic? The following are four life histories illustrating different ways in which some individuals become low or high ethnic. Some are more typical, but a study of the specifics of individual cases can provide a better insight into what has been presented in more general terms.

For most of the informants, as exemplified by the first two life histories, there was a great deal of continuity in their lives with regards to their ethnic identity and their degree of involvement with it. Adult high ethnics had been raised as high ethnics from childhood. Their parents preferred socializing mainly with Japanese Americans. As children and adolescents, the high ethnics themselves associated heavily with Japanese American peers. Through these interactions they learned Japanese American rules of conduct and styles of behavior.

Adult low ethnics associated mainly with nonJapanese Americans as children. Their parents either were not concerned that their children associate mainly with Japanese Americans or did not make the effort to provide them with opportunities to meet Japanese Americans. As a result, they learned nonJapanese American ways of human relations. They were often uncomfortable being with Japanese Americans whose behavior they did not understand.

The second two life histories represent those individuals who greatly changed their degree of ethnicity. Although they had been raised as high or low ethnic, for various reasons they decided to switch their group identification and made conscious efforts to learn the behavior patterns of their new group. These were adult decisions and permanent choices. They were not expressions of adolescent rebelliousness. Nor were they youthful experiments with different identities which a number of high ethnics felt they tried.

This decision to switch did not mean they could select just any ethnic identity. They had two basic choices - they could be ethnic Japanese American or they could be assimilating Japanese American. No single clear cut reason for this desire to change emerged, although those who switched into ethnicity seemed to feel they were misfits in mainstream society.

FOUR LIFE HISTORIES

Amy Hayashi: A High Ethnic Who Remained a High Ethnic

Amy Hayashi was born in a large midwestern city in 1953. She was the second of three children of *nisei* parents. Her parents owned a small "mom-and-pop" grocery store in a caucasian neighborhood and their clientele was nonJapanese American. The family lived on the second floor above the store and the children helped out in the store after school and on weekends.

Amy attended a public school where there were only two other Japanese American children besides her family. She was friends with both of them. All her other school friends were caucasian. They encountered some stares and verbal harassment ("Ching, chang, chinaman") from school mates, but she and her sister ignored such occurrences. They were taught by their parents to regard such people as ignorant. Her younger brother, however, got into fights over racial taunts.

Amy feels that her teachers held many stereotypes about Orientals. They expected her to be quiet, studious, and a good student. She was, but she resented the fact that they expected such behavior from her simply because she was Japanese American. She feels she and her siblings were forced into stereotypes because there were not enough Asians to counter them.

All of her mother's family lived in the same city. On weekends she played with her Japanese American cousins. They all got along well and today a number of them are still among her closer friends. Her family's social life revolved around the extended family and the city's Japanese American community. There were always large family gatherings on holidays and birthdays. They belonged to a Japanese American Christian church to which her cousins also went. They went to many of the Resettlers' Picnics for the Japanese Americans who had left the Relocation Camps and subsequently settled in the area. They also attended the annual *obon* festival.

On Saturdays the children went to Japanese language school where Amy met other *sansei* children. She did not make friends there, because to her it was just more school. When classes were over she would immediately return home to watch the cartoons on television and play with her cousins. Even though the family lived in a caucasian neighborhood, Amy had Japanese American as well as caucasian friends.

Her parents were divorced when she was about six years old. They sold the store and her mother supported the family by working as a beautician. Her father did not keep in contact with the family. As their extended family began to move to other states, one of her mother's sisters urged them to move to Gardena.

When Amy was eleven she left with her mother and siblings for Gardena. She was sad to leave her friends. On her last day of school she wanted to cry but didn't because she was afraid to show her emotions. In Gardena, they lived in a Japanese American section of the city where they still reside.

Amy had some minor problems adjusting to being around so many *sansei* children. She recalls feeling strange because she was no longer the only Japanese American. However, she found she liked not feeling unique and came home from school very excited. She relates the experience to *obon* festivals as a little girl around a lot of Japanese Americans for the first time.

Initially, her Japanese American classmates were not very friendly. Cliques had already been formed in grammar school and she was seen as an outsider. For several days they even refused to tell Amy their names. She very much wanted to be friends and was finally accepted into a group by continually hanging around them and being friendly.

Through high school, Amy's friends were mostly Japanese American. She dated Japanese Americans almost exclusively. At one point in high school, she wanted to date caucasians but her mother discouraged her and asked "Don't you know any nice Japanese boys?" She dated a caucasian once but had to sneak out of the house to do so. It made her unhappy and she did not date nonJapanese Americans again.

After graduation, Amy attended the University of California at Riverside where she lived in a dormitory. She was not happy there because of problems she encountered on the mainly caucasian campus. She had a confrontation with a girl who told her she thought the dormitory was only for white people. Her white roommate's mother was pleased that her daughter had a Japanese American roommate since Japanese are "clean and neat and study hard." Amy hated encountering this stereotype once again. She also found that eating Japanese food provoked curiosity or teasing from other students.

Amy transferred to the University of California at Los Angeles. She had not liked the all-white environment of Riverside and there were many Japanese American students at UCLA. Also, she wanted to study Japanese. She lived near campus with her older sister, took classes at the Asian American Studies Center and changed her major to East Asian Studies. She got to know many Japanese Americans through her classes and by working at the Asian American Studies Center.

While in high school, she had taught Sunday School at a Japanese American church. In college, she became involved in Agape, an Asian Christian Fellowship group. For the annual Japanese American religious retreat to Mt. Hermon, she helped to run a special camp for mentally retarded Asian children. During the year, the group of Japanese Americans connected with this project were in close contact with each other as they planned, raised funds and helped to counsel these children. She first met her fiance-to-be, also a high ethnic Born Again Christian *sansei* from Gardena, at Mt. Hermon. Jim came to the retreat with a mutual friend who introduced them to each other.

Amy graduated from college with a degree in East Asian studies. Her mother, however, felt her bachelor's degree had no economic value and pressured Amy into nursing. After obtaining her nursing degree, she worked as a nurse in a Gardena hospital. She was unhappy at the hospital and so also volunteered at a women's clinic in hopes of future employment there. She now works as a research assistant at an area university, which she enjoys much more. She continues to work part-time at her hospital job, although her mother would prefer that she be a full-time nurse.

Amy is planning her wedding for the coming summer. She had considered wearing a *kimono* but finally decided on the traditional American wedding gown. Even though they do not have much money she will follow the Japanese American wedding custom and have a formal dinner at a restaurant for her 200 guests.

She has visited Japan twice - once for four weeks and once for five weeks. The first time she was in Japan she underwent an identity crisis. She realized when she was with Japanese that "I'm not like you, I'm not Japanese;" she became aware of the American in herself.

When she was seven her grandfather had wanted to take her with him to live in Japan, but her mother had refused to give her up. While in Japan, she went to see his house. She also saw her Japanese cousins and wondered how she would have turned out had she lived in Japan. On the flight home, Amy cried because she felt she was leaving her original roots. Back in America, she felt truly Japanese American, the product of two cultures.

Amy consistently displays the Japanese American trait of strong family ties. Throughout her life her family, particularly her mother, has had a very strong influence on her. Both of her parents were very strict and her mother continued to be so after her divorce. Amy respects and admires her mother, who raised and sent three children to college while working variously as a beautician and a store clerk. Amy cares what her mother thinks and she sometimes feels badly because she feels she cannot meet her mother's expectations. She reluctantly stopped dating a seminary student whom her mother didn't like because she is basically an obedient daughter and feels that her mother knows what is best for her. While working as a nurse in Gardena she noticed that her Japanese American patients usually had their families gathered around their bedsides, which was less often the case with her caucasian patients. In addition, her extended family on her mother's side has helped her family, and even though many of them are now living elsewhere in the country everyone gets together for reunions and weddings. Many of her cousins are about the same age and they correspond with and visit each other.

Her family has the attitude that Japanese people are better, more clever and smarter. They use Japanese products at home and see them as superior to American manufactured products. Her mother has tried to teach her *ikebana* (Japanese flower arrangement) and Japanese cooking, but with little success. Amy is proud of being a Japanese American, although she feels that she sometimes is too predisposed towards anything Japanese American.

The other major influence in her life in Christianity. It is important to her that her husband be not only Japanese American but also Christian. She has always been involved in church or religious group activities and continued to be involved even in college, although she also went through a personal crisis when she questioned the existence of God. She has since emerged from that crises with an even stronger religious commitment. Although she has a strong identity as a Born Again Christian, an identity shared by many in the mainstream society, Amy has only gone to Japanese American or Asian American religious groups .and continues to do so today.

From an early childhood in the Midwest where she lived and attended school with caucasians and where her interactions with Japanese Americans was limited to the weekends and holidays (although these were important relationships), her contacts with Japanese Americans increased drastically after her family moved to Gardena. In Gardena she lived among and attended school with both Japanese Americans and caucasians. She became part of Japanese American friendship cliques and found she enjoyed the feeling of no longer being unique because she was the only Asian. Even in a large university like UCLA she was able to confine her friendships to other *sansei*. In her work as a nurse in Gardena she had some Japanese American patients, and her religious life is totally with other

Japanese Americans. Her memories of most of her experiences with caucasians - teachers, roommates, parents - are mainly negative, which helps to reinforce the preference for Japanese Americans which she initially learned at home. Today nearly all of her personal relationships, and certainly the more meaningful and satisfying ones, occur with Japanese Americans, particularly with Christian Japanese Americans. She has become so accustomed to being with Japanese Americans that she now feels very uncomfortable when she is the only Asian in a group of people. Her hopes are that her children - the *yonsei* generation - will also be high ethnics; that they, like their parents, will have mostly Japanese American friends and will eventually marry Japanese Americans.

Lisa Matsumoto: A Low Ethnic Who Remained a Low Ethnic

Lisa Matsumoto and her two younger brothers were born in a city adjacent to Los Angeles of a second-generation father and a third-generation mother. Lisa talks more often about her mother's side of the family and has very fond memories of her great grandfather who died when she was in high school. *Jichan* (Japanese for grandfather - she refers to her great grandparents as *jichan* and *bachan* and her grandparents as grandfather and grandmother) seems very unusual for a *nisei*. He spoke very good English, worked in real estate and was openly affectionate toward his grandchildren. She recalls that all the great grandchildren felt very comfortable with him, climbed on the bed with him to watch television, and used to tease him by doing such pranks as painting his fingernails different colors while he was sleeping. He gave Easter egg hunts every year for the children and freely passed out silver dollars to them. When Lisa was fifteen he suffered a heart attack on the golf course and died in a hospital shortly after all his great grandchildren were brought to his bedside to say goodbye.

After his death, *bachan*, who had been sickly for many years, went to live with her daughter, Lisa's grandmother. It eventually became too difficult to care for her and she went to a Japanese American retirement and convalescent home. Lisa's grandmother had married a *nisei-kibei* (who graduated from an American university and taught Japanese at UCLA for a number of years). Both grandparents are unusual since they are *nisei*, speak excellent English and are also very affectionate with their grandchildren. Lisa recalls that her grandfather gave his grandchildren a dollar for every A they made on their report cards, and took her to the Seattle World's Fair when she was accepted into an exclusive private school. He is not the remote, authoritarian Japanese grandfather figure, and Lisa often teases him. He plays with and hugs and kisses his year-old great grandson. He is now retired from his real estate business and does a lot of travelling with his wife, sometimes taking his four daughters and their husbands along to such places as Europe and Japan.

Lisa's parents eloped while they were still in college. Her mother was an undergraduate at the University of Southern California and her father was either in the School of Pharmacy or the Dental School; Lisa is uncertain which. He continued to attend school but found it impossible once Lisa and her brother were born. He now works as a gardener.

When Lisa was a year old the family purchased a house in a caucasian neighborhood. Over time other oriental families moved in so that from childhood Lisa had both caucasian and Japanese American friends. In elementary school she was always popular and belonged to the "in" group. In the sixth grade she was Student Council president. Although the older of her brothers belonged to a Japanese American boy scout troop and was involved in Japanese

American athletics, the only Japanese American organization she was involved with was the local Japanese American Presbyterian Church. However, when she was growing up this church held many activities jointly with caucasian churches. (More recently, it has confined its inter-church events to the five Japanese American Presbyterian churches in the area and the neighboring Japanese Buddhist Church). Neither she nor her two brothers went to Japanese language school. Both parents had been forced to go when they were children and so hated it that they decided not to do the same to their children.

Lisa's father is a quiet, easy-going person who gets along well with his in-laws. There is a lot of good-natured teasing and joking in the extended family. Lisa sees her mother as much more ambitious for her children. She wanted them to be accustomed to a more upper-class lifestyle so she took the lead in teaching her children etiquette - her sons learned to shake hands when very young and she made a point of always setting the dinner table as if for a formal dinner. Under her mother's urging Lisa went to a private girls' junior high school. Her parents' hopes were that she would graduate from there to a prep school and finally attend an Ivy League college.

Lisa was miserable at the girls' school. She disliked having to wear a uniform, and the majority of the students there were from a much higher economic background than her family. She recalls that after school chauffeurs in their limousines arrived to pick up their charges. Although there were only three Asian American students in the school, Lisa didn't mind and she only played with her caucasian classmates. In the eighth grade she was elected class president, but she still was unhappy there. Her main social life was now with her church's youth club. Giving in to the misery of her daughter, her mother allowed Lisa to return to public school once she graduated from the ninth grade.

For high school Lisa went back to public school where she already knew many of the students. Once again she was very popular and part of the "in" crowd. Her best friend was caucasian and she mainly dated caucasian boys. In her senior year she became a song girl. That year 60 people tried out in her high school for the eighteen positions on the cheering squad. Everyone elected was caucasian with the exception of Lisa and one other Asian American girl, and all the members formed a very close-knit group. Her mother also had her daughter try out for the Rose Bowl Queen tournament, which is dominated by caucasian contestants. Lisa did not win.

After high school Lisa first went to a nearby college because her father was reluctant to let his first-born leave home so soon. She transferred the next year to a college further from home and lived that year with her grandmother. She had planned to get her bachelor's degree but got married instead. Lisa had dated mostly caucasians in high school and through college, and the few Japanese Americans she had dated tended to be those who had been raised among caucasians, as she had been. Thus, they were more caucasian in their outlook and behavior. Her husband, an Orange county *sansei* of *nisei kibei* parents, was the only Japanese American she had dated who had Japanese American friends. Bob is tall for a Japanese American, athletic, attractive and has a very outgoing personality. When she first started dating him shortly after her graduation from high school he did not seem that "Japanesey" to her, but since they have gotten married she feels he has "gotten worse." She says that while they were dating he was trying to be the sophisticated man-of-the-world type, which she feels is not a Japanese American characteristic. Until they were married she never met his friends who were Japanese American.

After marriage Lisa worked as a secretary and her husband worked first in an insurance office and currently is a sales representative for a pharmaceutical company. Lisa hoped eventually to return to college to earn a bachelors degree but meanwhile, with two salaries, they lived well. They went out often, took skiing trips, and bought a Corvette, a car Bob had always wanted. They also returned to Lisa's childhood church, became more religious and eventually became Born Again Christians. About a year ago her husband was transferred to a Los Angeles office, so they moved to Gardena. This was the first time Lisa had ever lived among so many Japanese Americans. They presently have a one year old son and are expecting another child.

Lisa used to have only caucasian friends but because of her husband has begun to socialize more with his Japanese American friends. She often feels forced into doing this and occasionally resents it. She prefers to choose her friends as individuals rather than on the basis of whether they are Japanese American or not, and she dislikes and finds too constraining many Japanese American attitudes, behaviors and customs. Lisa feels that she is different in many ways from the Japanese Americans she has been meeting. She initially felt uncomfortable when around Japanese Americans, since she was not accustomed to it. She now feels less awkward, although she still feels more comfortable socializing with caucasians and has managed to form a few friendships with caucasians in Gardena. She and her husband have left their former church for a Japanese American church with a younger congregation. Lisa wanted to attend a caucasian church nearby that is religiously very active but her husband insisted on joining another Japanese American church.

Being raised in a basically nonJapanese middle class environment and under the influence of a close but somewhat atypical Japanese American extended family and a mother who desired more mainstream and upwardly mobile goals for her children, Lisa and her younger brothers were geared toward an assimilationist and caucasian lifestyle. Her brothers are still single and date caucasian girls.

Since Amy's marriage to a Japanese American who emerged as a high ethnic, she has been plunged against her will into a more Japanese American environment. However, she continues to be low ethnic in her attitudes. She conforms in behavior to Japanese American norms only to the extent that she must in order to maintain relationships, for she is basically a very sociable and outgoing person. On her own, without the presence of her husband, in a mixed group of Japanese Americans and caucasians she finds herself drawn to the caucasians and finds interacting with them to be "refreshing." Lisa does not dislike Japanese Americans *per se.* What she dislikes is insisting upon being Japanese American as an important criterion for interaction. Consequently, while she does not feel it is at all important that her children play with and marry Japanese Americans, she would not like them to reject socializing with Orientals simply because they are Oriental. Her hope is that her children will become more cosmopolitan in outlook than she feels her husband is, more like herself.

Sue Okamoto: A High Ethnic Who Became a Low Ethnic

Sue Okamoto, a doctor's wife and the mother of two sons, resides in one of the newer upper-middle class neighborhoods of Orange county. She was born and raised in Hawaii, the oldest of three children. Her parents were both *nisei*; her father was a carpenter and her mother a housewife and part-time seamstress. She grew up in a racially mixed neighborhood of Japanese, Chinese, Hawaiian, Portuguese and caucasian families, and her mother still resides in the same house today. She was very young when the

Japanese bombed Pearl Harbor and World War II began. Her only memories are of the black-out light bulbs they used in their home which were painted on the sides and only let light out through the bottom. Her mother later told her how frightened they were. The family burned all the pictures and belongings they had from Japan because they were afraid anything Japanese might be used in an attempt to incriminate them. Her mother talks about this with a real sense of loss.

After the war, Sue was sent to Japanese language school, which she disliked. She resented not being able to join a brownie troop or do other outside activities because her afternoons were taken up by more school. Her mother persuaded her to continue through elementary school and then she would be allowed to quit if she still disliked it. Today she knows very little Japanese.

Sue was a very rebellious child, which she feels is a very unJapanese American trait. Even when young she was very much for equality. In school the students were supposed to clean both their classroom and the bathrooms. The boys refused to help clean the bathrooms so the teacher had the girls clean both the girls' and the boys' bathrooms. Sue was very vocal in protesting this treatment as unfair and unequal. Her mother had to talk with her regarding the proper behavior for a female and asked her to at least not talk back to her teacher. So, to obey her mother, Sue reluctantly joined the other girls in cleaning both bathrooms, but she still thought it was very undemocratic. Throughout her childhood Sue was a very strong willed individual. Her mother wanted her to take lessons in flower arranging, classical dance, *koto* (Japanese musical instrument), brush painting, etc., which she felt was a proper education for a Japanese female, but her daughter refused for that very reason. Her mother, in efforts to get her oldest child to conform, would point out other Japanese girls to Sue and say, "See Barbara Ino? She's so neat and polite. Why can't you be like her?" This made her furious, since she hated being compared to other Japanese American girls.

In high school Sue continued to want to prove her equality with males. She wanted to join her high school debating team. Her mother, however, was against it since she felt it was not proper to be competing against males. Consequently, Sue wanted to do it even more. She enjoyed it, for here she could compete with males on equal grounds. She also went out of her way not to demonstrate ladylike behavior, so she would refuse any offers of help from males if she were carrying a heavy load of boxes and would not let them open doors for her.

This description of Sue's childhood should not give the reader the mistaken impression that she is an aggressive, vocal women's "libber" or an unattractive social misfit. Now in her early 30s, she is petite, well-groomed, pretty and soft-spoken. She feels she has become far more relaxed in her views.

Most of her friendships in Hawaii were with Japanese Americans, not because she deliberately sought them out but because there were simply more of them around. She felt she was more outgoing and explorative than most of her friends. She dated both Japanese Americans and nonJapanese Americans. She found it difficult to date nonJapanese Americans, however, because her mother wanted her to date Japanese Americans exclusively and to marry a Japanese American. After graduating from high school Sue went to the University of Hawaii where she met her husband-to-be. John, also a *sansei*, was different from other Japanese American males she had known - he was more talkative and articulate, more outgoing, and more aggressive. She feels she was attracted to him because he was so talkative, unlike her father who was extremely quiet. In addition, while meeting her mother's desire for her to marry a

Japanese American, he was the least Japanese of all the Orientals she'd known.

After graduating from the University of Hawaii with a bachelor's degree in Education Sue went to the University of Illinois for a master's degree in speech. She went there because it was close to the University of Chicago, where John was now going to medical school. She enjoyed the University of Illinois - this was her first experience away from home and she encountered no problems with prejudice. Once, on a train, a caucasian woman began to stare at her. Sue became uneasy believing that the woman did not like Orientals. When they got off, the woman approached her and told her she had been looking at her because she had such a nice smile. Sue now laughs at her anticipation of prejudice.

Even though she enjoyed being on her own, it still took some adjustment for Sue to move from an environment in which Japanese Americans were in the majority to an environment in which Japanese Americans were in the minority. She became close friends with a girl in her dormitory whom she had only known slightly in Hawaii. She would have liked to socialize more with Hawaiian Japanese Americans if there had been any. When she went to visit her fiance in Chicago she sought out people from Hawaii at Northwestern University and became friends with some of them.

After she got her master's degree in Speech Communications she and John were married. She taught in a Chicago junior high school while he finished his last year at medical school. They then moved to the East Coast, where he did his internship in a New York City hospital. Many of the patients were orthodox Jews, and they lived in an apartment building where many Jewish families also resided. Sue enjoyed the experience and socialized with Jewish friends they made. She also got to meet John's sister, who had married a Jew. This marriage was not accepted for a long time by the parents of either spouse.

They next moved to Stanford where her husband served his residency. Again they did not meet many Japanese Americans. After his four years at Stanford her husband served for two years in the navy, working at the Naval Hospital in Long Beach. By then their first son was born. Once John was out of the navy Sue wanted very badly to move back to Hawaii. Although she had enjoyed her years in Illinois, New York and California, she was still conscious of being a minority as a Japanese American on the continental United States and she wanted to return home where she could once again be part of the Japanese American majority. So they flew to Hawaii to see about the possibilities of jobs and housing. They returned very discouraged. Houses in Hawaii were scarce and expensive and job opportunities were not very promising. Her husband had talked with a number of doctors who were not happy in Hawaii. Their wives had been so homesick for Hawaii that their husbands had had to take any job in medicine, no matter how poor. Betty felt very strongly that her husband had to be satisfied professionally, even if it meant not being able to settle in Hawaii.

They reluctantly decided that John would work in a hospital in California, they would save what money they could, and after a year once again see what the situation was like. The job situation did not improve and after a year she discovered that California was not a bad place to live. They began to look for a house. They considered Torrance, which is adjacent to Gardena, because Sue wanted to live in an area where there were many Japanese Americans. However, they found the medical profession in Los Angeles was more established, and therefore more difficult to break into as a new doctor. They turned next to Orange county, even though there were fewer Japanese Americans, because the area was newer and rapidly developing, and as a result, easier to start a practice in.

The house they presently live in is the first home they have owned. Sue feels owning this house has made her feel more a part of the community of Newport Beach. On the cul-de-sac where they live there are families of many nationalities but no other Japanese Americans. Because neither she nor her children have experienced any problems with prejudice in their neighborhood living among Japanese Americans has become less and less important to her.

Sue's brother is married to a caucasian. Sue was extremely surprised that her parents came to the wedding and accepted their new daughter-in-law, since her mother had previously been so set against having nonJapanese Americans in the family. Later she talked with her mother about it and her mother apologized for the way she had acted with Sue. As she got older, Sue's mother explained, she had begun to realize how wrong her attitude was. Sue marvels at how her mother had decided that her attitude was hurtful and then set about to change it. Her mother and her caucasian daughter-in-law have a very warm relationship which Sue is envious of because she never got along very well with her Japanese American mother-in-law.

Sue is a member of a fairly exclusive Asian American women's social and service club in Orange county. She decided to join for a number of reasons: 1) since her husband had just started his practice in Orange county she hoped in this way to help widen their contacts and 2) she was interested in meeting other Orientals since the majority of her friends are now caucasian and she wanted friends who weren't all in medicine. This is the only Asian American organization she belongs to and she has not yet made any close friends from the organization with whom she socializes outside of club activities.

Sue, who was always somewhat of a rebel and more outgoing and adventuresome than her Japanese American friends, moved from a basically Japanese American environment as a child to a basically nonJapanese American environment as an adult. Although she initially had some problems adjusting to being a minority, and sought out other Hawaiian Japanese Americans for company, she was able to enjoy and meet different types of people during their moves to New York and California. She never encountered any problems with discrimination. However, in the back of her mind there was always the desire and the intention to return to Hawaii and be with other Japanese Americans. It was not until she was faced with the fact that living in Hawaii probably meant a drop in their standard of living, and in her husband's professional hopes, that Sue began to acknowledge what had been gradually occurring in her life over the years - she did not need to live with Japanese Americans and while nice, it was no longer of paramount importance to her that she interact with Japanese Americans. This change of attitude had been reinforced by the fact that as Japanese Americans neither she nor her family had encountered any problems of acceptance by the mainstream society.

In addition, Sue feels that in a number of ways she is different from many Japanese Americans. Some of these changes have resulted from her interactions with caucasians. One of the major changes has been in learning to be more physically demonstrative. When she was teaching at San Francisco State, one of the nonJapanese American professors there became a good friend of hers. He later told her about an incident when he was trying to talk with her and as he attempted to get closer she kept on backing off to put more distance between them. She had not been aware of this until her friend pointed it out. Now, sometimes when she has a strong desire to step backwards she tries not to because she realizes that it may be seen as too formal and unfriendly in the mainstream society. She has learned to hug her caucasian friends on greeting them and is now aware of her Jåpanese American friends backing off unconsciously when Sue tries to do the same with them. Another good friend who is also nonJapanese American has helped her to become less defensive about being a minority and she now laughs about her past attitudes. Sue feels that the more ethnic people are more sensitive to real or imagined racial slights than she is.

Sue is trying to socialize her two sons in ways that she feels are more American, such as learning to be freer in terms of physical contact and to place less reliance on their parents as authority figures and more reliance on themselves as responsible persons. She is not trying deliberately to make her children totally unJapanese American, for there is much about her childhood she likes. Rather, she feels she is adding on to already established patterns in areas that she feels were lacking in her own socialization. To her it is this adding on that has moved the socialization of her boys more towards American patterns. Except for personality differences she does not see any differences between her sons and their nonJapanese American playmates in terms of race. Currently, her children do not have any regular Japanese American playmates, nor does she see it as particularly important. She feels that she can relate to people as people rather than as racial or cultural categories and she would like her children to learn this as well. It is also important that they have some association with Japanese American children, but they have this through family activities her club sponsors. While Sue thinks it would be nice if her sons married Japanese Americans, of far more importance to her is their economic status. Regardless of their ethnic background she prefers that they not marry women of a lower economic status or women who have had considerably less education than she assumes her sons will have.

Jerry Takasue: A Low Ethnic Who Became a High Ethnic

Jerry Takasue, a politically radical *sansei* activist, was born in metropolitan Los Angeles of second-generation parents, the oldest of four sons.

His mother had a strong influence on him until her death a few years ago. She was quite unusual for a *nisei* woman. Being born late in her own mother's life, she was raised primarily by her older brother who owned a bar and grill in Cleveland in an area that was mainly white and black in racial composition. As a result, she was more Americanized in attitude and behavior than her *nisei* peers. Her best friend was a prostitute. In high school she refused to date Japanese American boys. Her parents, concerned about this, forced her to join Japanese American organizations and agreed to let her marry Jerry's father, the first Oriental she fell in love with, even though he was a Japanese American of Okinawan ancestry.

Of the two, Jerry's mother was far less "Japanesey" than his father. His father, like most *nisei*, was more reticent, while his mother was less restrained in the expression of her feelings. She would openly hug and kiss her husband even though it embarrassed him, and she did the same with her four sons. She stressed independence and individuality whereas his father was concerned with how Jerry's behavior would affect the family's reputation. She drank, smoked and cursed and was more tolerant of such behavior in her children, feeling they were capable of using their own judgement not to go to excesses.

The family lived in South Los Angeles in a working class neighborhood that was initially a mixture of caucasian and Japanese American families but then gradually changed to mainly black families. Jerry went to a racially mixed elementary school where he first developed his dislike of Japanese Americans. He doesn't know why but he faced a good deal of ostracism by his Japanese American classmates. He did not do well academically although he is very intelligent. He also got into trouble because, unlike the other Japanese American children, he was very open in saying what he felt. In addition, because of continuing health problems, his opportunities to compete in sports were limited.

In junior high school Jerry continued to socialize mostly with whites and blacks and found this to be a positive experience. In addition, his grades began to improve and his father stopped pressuring him, so he enjoyed junior high school. However, he began to fight with Japanese American boys, was thrown out of classes for his behavior and developed a reputation as a troublemaker in the Japanese American community. He was told by a *sansei* teacher of his that he was a blacksheep. There were racial problems beginning in school between blacks and Japanese Americans, but Jerry never encountered any problems with black students. He was attacked by Japanese American and white students and developed negative feelings about these groups. At this time, the family's neighborhood was becoming very rough - they were in the first curfew zone during the Watts riots of 1965. They moved to Redondo Beach, a white area. His father had wanted to move to Gardena because he was worried that his sons were not meeting Japanese American girls, but his mother felt living near so many Japanese Americans would be too constraining. Jerry and his brothers were very reluctant to leave their school. For a while Jerry bicycled six miles after school back to his former neighborhood to be with his old friends. His father placed him back half a year in junior high school because at this time the Viet Nam war was in progress and he wanted Jerry to still be in high school when he turned eighteen. Because their new junior high school was exclusively white in composition, his younger brothers had some problems with racial taunts and jokes. However, since Jerry was now bigger and older than most of his classmates, he did not encounter too many problems.

In high school, however, he was made to feel different by his classmates because he was Japanese American. The surfing look was the current fad - white t-shirts, pale blue jeans, tennis shoes, and long bleached hair - but Jerry and his brothers were not allowed to dress in this fashion. When December 7th arrived, his white classmates constantly reminded him of it, which angered Jerry. He wanted to feel accepted but, instead, he was made to feel different.

In retrospect, Jerry feels that the majority of the incidences of prejudice were not intentionally hostile but were due to ignorance. He became so overly sensitive, however, that he got to a point where he was looking for any sign of prejudice, perhaps even where none was meant. He would not let any incident of suspected discrimination go unchallenged. Even though his friends were caucasian, he began to hate whites as a group.

Meanwhile, efforts were being made by some *sansei* students to break out of the conservative mold of their parents and, like the Black Panther and Chicano movements before them, the started a more politically radical and activist Japanese American and Asian American organization. At the end of his sophomore year, feeling he was a misfit, Jerry had begun to look elsewhere for acceptance. The Yellow Brotherhood with its militant and activist stance appealed to him. Suffering from racism he turned to a group that was openly protesting racism against Asians and other minorities. Both on and off campus he became involved with activist topics - he brought a draft counselor to speak at school, arranged for the showing of anti-war films, and joined various Japanese American community organizations. During this period he began to have problems with drug and alcohol abuse and was in constant conflict with his father. Previously he only dated caucasians.

Shortly before he graduated from high school Jerry began to date Asians. Previously he had only dated caucasians. After high school, while continuing to do volunteer work in Gardena and working at a full-time job, he began to socialize more intensively with Asian Americans. He socialized less often now with his caucasian friends and only maintained the relationships that were close ones. In order to have both Asian and caucasian friends Jerry found he had to operate in two separate social circles. He was criticized by his Asian peers for having caucasian friends while his caucasian friends did not understand Japanese American ways.

Jerry also found that he had to modify his behavior so as to be accepted by his Asian American and Japanese American peers. What he had always been used to doing - speaking up, being aggressive and even confrontive - he had to struggle to change. It was difficult for him and he often felt at a disadvantage because he was unfamiliar with Japanese American norms, so he was often not certain what type of behavior was expected of him. But he persevered and over the years has been able to bring his behavior into the acceptable Japanese American range. People in Gardena have noticed the change and comment on how much he's "quieted down."

Jerry now feels that he is less comfortable with the few caucasian friends he still sees occasionally, has lost some of the skill at white interaction patterns he used to have, and where previously he was accustomed to being the only Asian in a crowd he now feels uncomfortable to be in such a situation. Sometimes he regrets some of the changes he sees in himself, but he has been willing to make the efforts to fit into the Japanese American community because his self-identity is now very much bound up with being a Japanese American and an Asian American.

A few years ago Jerry moved into an apartment in Gardena and has been working in a job counseling center for Asians. His current girlfriend is a Gardena *sansei* and he socializes almost totally with Japanese Americans and other Asian Americans.

Since the sudden death of his mother, which badly upset the family, he has come to be a unifying force in his family. His father has come to rely on his advice and help although they still have strong disagreements at times. Although he feels that he and his brothers are different from most Japanese Americans, due to their mother's influence, he is also beginning to find more similarities between his father and himself than he had previously realized existed.

Jerry's three younger brothers are not as involved with being Japanese American as he is. He feels that they did not turn against the caucasian society they were raised in because they had more stable peer groups than the people he got involved with. They also seemed to be less sensitive to any racial taunts they might have encountered. Jerry, however, had had problems of acceptance ever since he entered elementary school. When he was still made to feel different in high school, he began to seek out Japanese Americans, a group he once disliked. He could not change his race but he could and was willing to modify his behavior in order to be accepted. His brothers, on the other hand, have no desire to modify their behavior, so they do not feel accepted by the Gardena Japanese Americans. They do not date Japanese Americans. While his youngest brother's best friend is Japanese American, he is like himself - an Americanized Japanese American.

SUMMARY

For all of the four individuals described above a sense of comfortably fitting into their surroundings, of sharing or wanting to share the same expectations and rules of behavior with the people they chose to interact with were important factors in their degree of involvement with their ethnic identity. Subtle as they may be to the naive observer, significant differences do exist between the rules of human relations found in the larger more generalized American culture and those found in the more enclosed third-generation Japanese American subculture.

Because a knowledge and understanding of one or the other style of human relations results from a long socialization process, usually beginning in childhood, most informants in their own adult lives followed the orientation of their parents. That is, adult high ethnics such as Amy Hayashi generally were raised in high ethnic families while adult low ethnics such as Lisa Matsumoto grew up in far more of a mainstream environment. It is the rare individual who can comfortably, skillfully and unselfconsciously operate on a close, personal level in both styles of behavior. As a result, these *sansei* tended to remain with what they knew best and, therefore, felt more comfortable with.

It was more unusual to encounter individuals who, as adults, had consciously changed their ethnic orientation. The few such individuals had definite reasons for their willingness to, in essence, resocialize themselves to a new style of interaction with others. For the high ethnics who became low ethnics, such as Sue Okamoto, the process occurred gradually and was even to a great extent not a conscious decision until the change was all but complete. As long as they encountered no problems of acceptance by the mainstream society, found their increasing social interactions with nonJapanese Americans to be enjoyable and even enlightening and were themselves willing to change some of their behavior patterns so as to comfortably accept and deal with mainstream norms, there was less of a desire on their part to return to the ethnicity of their childhood. In addition, a physical removal to another city or state where distance made it less convenient for them to remain in close contact with their family and Japanese American friends was an important aid in their gradual social and psychological removal from their Japanese American community. Seeing their old Japanese American friends less, it was easier for them to increase their contacts with nonJapanese Americans and to seek the benefits they saw existing in the larger society.

Even more unusual were individuals, such as Jerry Takasue, who from being a low ethnic child and adolescent became a high ethnic adult. The process of resocialization to Japanese American norms appears to be a more difficult task than the process of resocialization to mainstream norms. By the third and fourth generations considerable familiarity and facility with American culture has been acquired. The task of learning the mainstream style of interactions is not the overwhelming one faced by the immigrant generation to whom everything American - language, food, religion, etc. - was new. In addition, when compared to the Japanese American interaction pattern, mainstream American norms of human relations appear to be more informal, less complex and more fluid. This is felt to be the case by many of the informants in this study. Many feel that Japanese American friendships are deeper and longer lasting than American ones but are also far more difficult to establish and take more care to maintain. Consequently, the few *sansei* encountered in this study who attempted successfully or unsuccessfully to become high ethnics reported a good deal of difficulty in trying to learn the appropriate norms and to modify their behavior accordingly so as to be accepted by other high ethnic *sansei*. These individuals had to want to become part of a Japanese American group or community strongly enough that they were willing to persist in spite of numerous rebuffs.

As with the high ethnics who became low ethnics, their reasons for their decision varied. The sample is too small to make any generalization except that all of them felt that somehow they were misfits who did not fit comfortably into the larger society. Even though all of them were able to function effectively with nonJapanese Americans they felt different, a feeling which they disliked. They chose, therefore, to limit most of their social and more meaningful relations to other Japanese Americans. In this way they were no longer different physically. However, they had to work to modify their behavior so that they could feel comfortable and acceptable socially.

CONCLUSION

PURPOSES OF THE RESEARCH

A major question of this study was why does ethnicity continue to remain salient for later generations of former immigrant groups? This question is of particular interest with reference to Japanese Americans, an ethnic group in a hospitable environment highly conducive to assimilation. For these later generations, there are no obvious barriers such as a divergent language or culture which would make it difficult for them to function in the general American society. They are highly acculturated; the homeland culture of their grandparents and great-grandparents is as foreign to them as it would be to any other American. As a group they are economically successful. Their occupations cover a wide range extending even into areas of the economy where ethnic networks may be of little assistance. They blend well into American society; the vast majority do not want to remain obviously culturally distinct from the mainstream society.

These later generation Japanese Americans do not face any widespread hostility or intentional discrimination. They may recall stories of beatings and lynchings, of signs in windows saying "No Japs or Chinks allowed", of educational and occupational opportunities and housing areas that were closed to previous generations but these happened many years ago to their grandparents. For these later generations, prejudice is the exceptional occurrence. It does not prevent them from participating fully in American life, nor does it provide a strong impetus for defensively banding together. Why, then, does ethnicity persist for later generations such as the third- and fourth-generation Japanese Americans?

A second question arose from the first. Francis (1976) distinguishes between primary and secondary ethnic groups. A primary ethnic group is usually formed by the processes of nationalization within a given state population. And, thus, is transferred into another environment as a viable corporate unit. It continues to function in the host society as an essentially comprehensive subsociety capable of satisfying all the basic social needs of its members. A secondary ethnic group, on the other hand, is generally formed through migration, usually across international boundaries. Ethnics of this type enter their host society as isolated individuals or as small groups of migrants. They are, consequently, are far more dependent on their host society for the satisfaction of almost all their basic needs.

Japanese Americans, like most American ethnic groups, may be classified as a secondary ethnic group. Given the pervasiveness and the strong influence of their host society, how did the initial aggregation of Japanese American individuals manage to separate themselves in some part from the rest of American society in the formation of secondary ethnic groups? With the further intermeshing of later generations into American society, this separation becomes much more difficult; how does ethnicity persist for individuals of these later generations?

REASONS FOR ETHNICITY

In attempting to arrive at some answers, we made an important distinction between ethnic category and ethnic group. Anyone born of Japanese American parents is a member of the Japanese American ethnic category. The ethnic group, on the other hand, is the functioning social unit of Japanese Americans who are more or less closely networked with other Japanese Americans. It is necessary to learn the distinctive ways of the ethnic groups in order to be accepted as a member. Many researchers have studied members of the ethnic category as though they were all members of the ethnic group. The first-generation Japanese Americans were far more homogeneous and, in order to survive in a new culture, more unified in their activities. The later generations had the economic security, the knowledge and the skills to expand further into, what was to them, their native culture. Researchers did not interpret this increased diversity as reflecting a greater personal freedom of choice in a more accepting environment for individuals of ethnic categories. Rather, they assumed that the change from homogeneity to heterogeneity was a sign of impending assimilation and of the end of ethnicity.

However, as Hosokawa, Corrado, Maykovich and others have found, within an ethnic category, there are different types of ethnic identification and degrees of commitment to an ethnic identity. In this study of the *sansei* and *yonsei*, they displayed a continuum of degrees of identification and affiliation with Japanese Americans. Those with a smaller degree of identification - the low ethnics - were more concerned with assimilation into mainstream society. The high ethnics preferred to keep the noninstrumental parts of their lives separated from the nonJapanese American community. When high ethnics and low ethnics were compared, significant differences in attitudes and behavior were found. To speak, therefore, of all *sansei* as equally ethnic is a confusing simplification.

Since the concerned was with the Japanese American ethnic group rather than the ethnic category, a definition of ethnicity was needed - what it meant to belong to an ethnic group. As a result of the initial part of this work among the Japanese Americans, ethnicity was delimited as comprised of two factors: 1) a psychological/cultural element in which an individual in a plural society identifies with a group of the same cultural origin as his own. Inherent in this is his recognition that he and the group he identifies with differ in meaningful ways from other groups, and the acknowledgement that these differences stem ultimately from differences of cultural heritage; and 2) a behavioral/social component in which the individual uses elements of the ethnic culture, consciously and unconsciously, to identify himself as a member of the group. This is also a social phenomenon in that the ethnic behavior is based on the shared expectations and rules of behavior of the ethnic group. The possession of one element is insufficient to determine degree of ethnicity - it is the combination which makes a person a high ethnic.

The questionnaire based on this definition did not center on traditional Japanese folk culture. It did not elicit a material culture trait list, but focused on the social nature of ethnicity. Questions concentrated on types of activities and behaviors done with other people, preferences for interacting with one group of people or another, comfort or discomfort felt in relating to different groups of people, and perception of differences or similarities between the subject and other people.

The third-generation Japanese Americans sampled displayed a range of levels of ethnicity and of the desire to be ethnic. This enabled us to clearly distinguish the attitudes and behavior of the high ethnics from that of the low ethnics. High ethnics had a stronger psychological identification as Japanese Americans and were more likely to see more differences between themselves as Japanese Americans and the rest of American society. They took part in more activities that brought them into contact mainly with Japanese Americans while limiting the presence of nonJapanese Americans.

They were also more concerned that their children remain ethnic and placed a greater importance on living with other Japanese Americans than did the low ethnics.

Once the distinction was made between high and low ethnics, the concerned was with why some Japanese Americans were high ethnic and why others were low ethnic. This issue was first approached from the perspective of personal choice - why does this person want to be ethnic and why does that person not want to be ethnic?

In pursuing answers to this question one major theme appeared and reappeared - that of comfort within an ethnic style. Cultural differences between high ethnic *sansei* and nonJapanese Americans were found, particularly in the area of interpersonal relations. These differences do much to make a person feel comfortable or uncomfortable when interacting with others. A high ethnic Japanese American tends to feel comfortable when the people he interacts with agree on and follow the same rules of human relations, and tends to feel uncomfortable when the rules are different from what he is accustomed to. These high ethnic *sansei* are willing to adapt their behavior to meet their political and economic needs and, in fact, in these areas, want to be a part of the larger society. However, they also want to keep an area of their lives separate in which they can "be themselves" with other Japanese Americans.

The differences that cause them to want to remain separate are learned behaviors and attitudes. They are so important that *sansei* who have not learned the "correct" behavior do not fit well into the ethnic group. They are stamped with the label "banana" and rejected by the high ethnic Japanese Americans. Likewise, the few caucasians who have fully learned the Japanese American style of social interaction are accepted by these *sansei* and given the complementary label of "egg" - i.e., white on the outside but yellow on the inside.

The ways in which high ethnic Japanese Americans differ from nonJapanese Americans form a complex pattern of behaviors. These behaviors, however, may not be readily apparent, particularly to the outsider with whom contact is limited and confined to certain areas of life. In general, high ethnic *sansei* seem to feel they are less aggressive and assertive in interaction and verbally less skillful than nonJapanese Americans. They believe they exhibit a greater sensitivity to the thoughts and feelings of others. They have a tendency to avoid dealing openly with problems in relationships or, if necessary, to use indirect methods in dealing with them. They are concerned with saving face and where the potential for disagreement exists, structure interaction patterns so as to leave acceptable and graceful ways out. High ethnic *sansei* seem to be more polite and courteous in structured situations, and less friendly (more formal) and outgoing than nonJapanese Americans. They are less individualistic, find comfort as a member of the ethnic group and are willing to conform to group standards to retain that comfort. The resultant emphasis on group conformity tends to make members less tolerant of individual differences; tight, although indirect, social control assures adherence to group norms. The high value placed on reciprocal obligation and generosity distinguishes them from nonJapanese Americans, but also operates to limit interaction outside of the group.

None of the elements of this behavioral complex is immediately obvious to outsiders. Frequently, even *sansei* are unable to articulate them, although they do recognize that they exist. These distinctive behavior patterns are normally learned first at home and reinforced and elaborated through interaction with other Japanese Americans. They are usually not consciously or deliberately taught and are so deep-rooted that they continue to be passed on despite the pervasive influence of the mainstream culture.

These ethnic behaviors are subject to change in form or content to fit the needs of each successive generation. The ways in which the first-generation Japanese Americans differ from nonJapanese Americans are not the same ways in which the second- or third-generation differs. What is significant for ethnicity is that the high ethnics in each generation continue to see themselves as different from the mainstream society.

These divergent behaviors must be viewed as Japanese American rather than Japanese. It is misleading to compare *sansei* with either present day Japanese nationals or the traditional Japanese folk culture of the early Japanese immigrants in an attempt to demonstrate their loss of ethnicity. The *sansei* differentiate between themselves and other Americans; they do not care how different they are from the Japanese, although they recognize that they are. In addition, many of these behaviors are unique to Japanese Americans and are not found in Japan. The Japanese Americans are a group with a cultural background different from that of the comparable age group in Japan. Finally, many of the divergent elements may have originally sprung from the culture of Meiji Japan, but they are not necessarily "peripheral remnants of immigrant ethnicity, [which are] not vital forms" as Patterson states (1979:104). As was seen in the discussion of the Japanese American system of reciprocal obligation, traditional forms can still be vital parts of ethnicity for later generations albeit changed in function, meaning or structure.

As well as comfort there are also some political and economic benefits that can be gained through the advocacy of Japanese American or Asian American based interest groups. With the relatively small size of the Japanese American population, however, benefits tend to be minor as compared with gains due to individual efforts. Their numbers are insufficient to achieve any major political presence except on the local community level. Efforts to gain more power through their organization as an Asian American/Pacific Islander coalition have proven somewhat more fruitful in terms of state and federal funding, but many problems emerge because of the extreme diversity within such an artificially organized group. Such a grouping does not hold much personal relevancy for most *sansei*.

Ethnicity for high ethnic *sansei* is much more than a complex of empty symbols devoid of social content. Their ethnicity is of a more old-fashioned type - they live it rather than simply use it; their Japanese Americanness is vital and dynamic.

THE MAINTENANCE OF ETHNICITY

As a group, the *sansei* are economically successful, highly acculturated and interact with nonJapanese Americans on an equal footing. To assimilate would be a relatively easy process; to remain ethnic requires a certain amount of effort. In addition, the presence of nonJapanese Americans in Japanese American circles is disruptive of the patterned and controlled ethnic behavior. Friendship networks, organizational affiliations and the system of reciprocal obligation provide effective means for Japanese Americans to keep in communication and to interact with each other. At the same time, they exclude nonJapanese Americans from active participation in the noninstrumental, and to these Japanese Americans, the more personally meaningful and satisfying parts of their lives. Consequently, while the Japanese Americans may live in neighborhoods that are mainly nonJapanese American in composition, attend schools with classmates who are mostly nonJapanese American, and work in nonJapanese American companies with mostly nonJapanese American colleagues, they can, if they so choose, create a Japanese American environment where they can socialize as Japanese Americans with other Japanese Americans.

This partitioning of an important aspect of their lives from mainstream society serves to reinforce and perpetuate these differences. The areas of difference that the high ethnics emphasize are those that deal with human relations. The partitioned areas are those where individuals deal most intensively, intimately and informally with others. Obviously, interacting mainly with those with the same norms and behaviors gives an individual less opportunity to learn, become skillful in and feel comfortable using a different style of human relations. As a result, the separation helps to reinforce the differences.

It should be repeated that these differences need not remain static; ethnic subcultures change and evolve over time. The significance for the persistence of ethnicity lies in the fact that, whatever the differences may be, differences do exist between the ethnic group and whatever other group it is comparing itself with. As long as an ethnic group is successful in preventing its assimilation into a larger social system, the chances are good that differences will remain; as long as differences remain and the differences are valued, the chances are good that the group will desire to protect itself from total assimilation.

ON BECOMING ETHNIC OR NONETHNIC

In the majority of cases those individuals who were raised as high ethnics remained high ethnics as adults, and those individuals who were raised as low ethnics remained low ethnics as adults. However, there were individuals who broke away from the group and attempted, with varying degrees of success, to cross over from high ethnicity to low ethnicity, as there were low ethnic individuals who sought to become high ethnics. These attempts at crossing over occurred as adults and were seen by the individuals as permanent commitments. The commitments were regarded as being of a different order than the adolescent rebellions and experiments with identity which a number of *sansei* said they had engaged in when younger, before they had taken on the responsibilities of jobs and families.

The individuals in the sample who had crossed over each had their own personal reasons. No general explanation emerged, although it is possible to point out a potentially fruitful direction for further investigation. The explanation may be in specific personality characteristics. Low ethnic individuals who have characteristics similar to or compatible with high ethnics - may feel uncomfortable and that they are misfits in the nonethnic environment. Upon discovering their similarity to high ethnics, they may be drawn to Japanese American ethnicity, become willing to learn the appropriate behavior and move from ethnic category member to ethnic group member. Likewise, low ethnic individuals may feel too restricted by *sansei* norms of behavior. If they feel a choice is possible, they may be drawn to assimilation. The data from this study are insufficient to make this explanation anything more than conjecture.

CONCLUDING REMARKS

As we have seen, ethnicity exists for the highly acculturated, well educated, economically advantaged, socially accepted third-generation Japanese Americans. Ethnicity is not merely a stage on the path to an inevitable assimilation. It is not a measuring stick upon which to gauge how "American" a group has become. It is a theoretical construct which helps to explain dynamic social processes.

Ethnicity has been conceived of as allowing a measure of choice, rather than as an imperative or as an ascriptive status, and characterized it by a range of affiliation. We have also separated the concept of ethnic category from that of ethnic group. To clarify this issue, ethnicity was defined as comprised of two aspects - a psychological/cultural one and a behavioral/social one. Thus it was possible to view ethnicity as a continuum and to differentiate between high and low ethnics in terms of activities and behaviors, interaction preferences and patterns, and values and attitudes.

In the case of the *sansei* we have seen that to be ethnic requires a certain amount of work; especially in the suburbs it takes time and effort to establish and maintain ethnic networks. One of the major reasons ethnicity persists for them is the comfort elicited in situations where values and behavioral expectations are held in common. Closely tied to comfort is ethnic style - less the particular actions of the individual than the way in which he conducts his life and relates to the world and to others.

It was proposed that becoming a high ethnic Japanese American required both the acquisition of the appropriate behavior and the establishment and intensification of Japanese American social networks. Friendship networks and organizational networks were important for maintaining ethnicity, although their initial order of development varied according to the characteristics of the setting. For those living in areas of fairly high Japanese American residential concentration, friendship networks often preceded organizational networks. In fact, the latter often grew directly out of the former. In the suburbs where residential concentration of Japanese Americans is low, it was usually first necessary to become established in organizational networks, from which friendship networks evolved. The systems of reciprocal obligation served to maintain these networks, to intensify social and personal relationships between kin, friends and acquaintances and to foster a sense of community. Reciprocal obligation, ethnic style and discrepancies between Japanese Americans and nonJapanese Americans effectually excluded nonJapanese Americans from the expressive realms of Japanese American life.

Ethnicity remains alive for later generations of Japanese Americans. The motivation and form may have changed over the generations, but it continues because it is important for high ethnics - it is something they choose to perpetuate. This research can provide a base for studying later generations of other ethnic groups. Do the differences between high and low ethnic Japanese Americans exist for other groups? Is comfort as important a reason to others for the persistence of ethnicity as it is for Japanese Americans? Are the mechanisms by which Japanese American ethnic networks are established and maintained the same, or equivalent, as in other ethnic groups? The answers to questions such as these would help in understanding the nature of ethnicity and its importance in the construction of a social reality for ethnic groups operating in plural societies.

APPENDIX A

SUMMARY OF SIGNIFICANT DIFFERENCES BETWEEN HIGH AND LOW ETHNICS

TABLE 1

SUMMARY OF SIGNIFICANT DIFFERENCES
PSYCHOLOGICAL IDENTIFICATION

	Low Ethnics	High Ethnics	Test and significance
1) Identifies self as Japanese American before American	56%	100%	X_c^2=11.655**
2) "Americanness"-"Japanese Americanness/Japaneseness" scale (4 point scale)	x=1.80	x=2.48	t=-4.13***
3) Importance that some sort of Japanese American identity continue to exist (4 point scale)	x=2.52	x=3.88	t=-7.29***
4) How upset if Japanese Americans intermarried to such an extent that eventually no "pure" Japanese American (4 point scale)	x=1.60	x=3.24	t=-6.64***
5) How much feel fate is bound up with fate of other Japanese Americans (4 point scale)	x=1.92	x=2.96	t=-4.92***
6) How much feel fate is bound up with fate of other Americans	x=2.56	x=2.40	t=0.62
7) Fate bound up more with other Japanese Americans, other Americans, or equally (Figures indicate percent who felt fate bound up more with other Japanese Americans)	8%	48%	X_c^2=17.610***
8) Would feel insulted if major newspaper insulted Japanese Americans	64%	92%	X_c^2= 4.195*
9) Would feel pleased if major newspaper praised Japanese Americans	68%	96%	X_c^2= 4.878*
10) Feel closer to people of Japanese ancestry than to persons of other backgrounds.	36%	92%	X_c^2=14.670***
11) How important a part does the fact of being Japanese American play in life (4 point scale)	x=2.28	x=3.60	t=-8.95***

* $p \leq .05$

** $p \leq .01$

*** $p \leq .001$

TABLE 2

OCCASIONS ON WHICH ONE FEELS MORE JAPANESE AMERICAN OR AMERICA[illegible]

Occasion	Low Ethnics	High Ethnics	Significant Difference
1) No occasion	2 (8%)	0 (0%)	
2) When with other Japanese Americans	13 (52%)	19 (76%)	
3) When with nonJapanese Americans	10 (40%)	21 (84%)	X_c^2=8.489**,ø
4) Religious occasions	4 (16%)	10 (40%)	
5) Japanese cultural events	19 (76%)	25 (100%)	X_c^2=4.735*,ø=
6) Political events	2 (8%)	8 (32%)	
7) Occupation	6 (24%)	13 (52%)	
8) Recreational, social events	7 (28%)	16 (64%)	X_c^2=5.153*,ø=
9) Family occasions	15 (60%)	18 (72%)	
10) Organizational meetings	6 (24%)	18 (72%)	X_c^2=10.786**,ø=
11) Unfamiliar cities, situations	12 (48%)	20 (80%)	X_c^2=4.253*,ø

* $p \leq .05$

** $p \leq .01$

[a]High ethnics are more likely to be aware of being Japanese American w they are with nonJapanese Americans than are low ethnics

[b]High ethnics are more likely to feel Japanese American when they ar Japanese cultural events than are low ethnics, although this type of event tend elicit feelings of Japanese American identity for both groups more than any ot category.

[c]Those whose ethnicity is salient are more likely to feel more Japa American at recreational or social events than those whose ethnicity is less sal

[d]High ethnics tend to feel more Japanese American at meetings conducted an organization, i.e. business company, service club, etc., than do low ethnics

[e]Those to whom their ethnicity is highly important are more likely to be s conscious of their Japanese Americanness when they are in unfamiliar citie situations than are those to whom ethnicity is less important.

TABLE 3

SUMMARY OF SIGNIFICANT DIFFERENCES
PERCEPTION OF DIFFERENCES

	Low Ethnics	High Ethnics	Significant Difference
1) More American or Japanese American/Japanese in outlook on life (4 point scale)	x=1.92	x=3.28	*t*=−5.99***
2) More American or Japanese American/Japanese in values and beliefs (4 point scale)	x=2.08	x=3.16	*t*=−4.95***
3) More American or Japanese American/Japanese in way of relating to people (4 point scale)	x=1.80	x=3.00	*t*=−5.76***
4) Feel more comfortable with Japanese American or nonJapanese Americans (5 point scale)	x=2.96	x=4.20	*t*=−5.29***
5) More American or Japanese American/Japanese in way of raising children (4 point scale)	x=2.12	x=3.16	*t*=−5.55***

* $p \leq .05$

** $p \leq .01$

*** $p \leq .001$

TABLE 4

SUMMARY OF SIGNIFICANT DIFFERENCES
ACTIVITIES AND BEHAVIOR

	Low Ethnics	High Ethnics	Test and significance
1) Importance of associating with other Japanese Americans (4 point scale)	x=1.72	x=3.48	t=-11.03***
2) Proportion of friends who are Japanese American (figures show percent indicating more than half)	36%	72%	X^2= 8.673*
3) Dating (figures show percent indicating "mostly" or "all" Japanese Americans)	40%	84%	X^2=10.272**
4) More likely to make charitable contribution if asked by Japanese American	12%	80%	X^2=20.612***
5) More likely to make contribution if Japanese American charity	20%	88%	X^2=20.662***
6) Percent of yearly contributions to Japanese American/Japanese organizations or causes			X^2= 9.413*
7) More likely to vote for a political candidate if he/she Japanese American (4 point scale)	x=1.96	x=2.92	t=-3.51***
8) More willing to use influence to help a Japanese American get a job than a nonJapanese American	x=1.28	x=2.88	t=-6.38***
9) Subscribe to Japanese or Japanese American periodicals or newspapers	12%	48%	X^2= 6.095*
10) Attend *obon* festivals			X^2=10.012*
11) Attend *Nisei* Week activities			X^2=12.486**
12) Attend Japanese American carnivals			X^2=10.020*
13) Attend Japanese American ceremonial dinners			X^2=10.020*
14) Attend Japanese American social dances			X^2=25.915***
15) Attend Japanese American sports events			X^2=19.200***
16) Attend Japanese or Japanese American entertainment shows			X^2=19.500***
17) Attend educational talks by or about Japanese Americans			X^2=21.200***
18) Attend picnics, beach parties, etc., with mostly Japanese Americans			X^2=14.600**
19) Take trips (longer than 1 day) given by Japanese American or Japanese organizations			X^2=12.381**

* $p \leq .05$

** $p \leq .01$

*** $p \leq .001$

TABLE 5

SUMMARY OF SIGNIFICANT DIFFERENCES
PASSING ON THE HERITAGE

	Low Ethnics	High Ethnics	Test and significance
1) Importance that children identify as Japanese American (4 point scale)	x=2.24	x=3.72	*t*=-7.46***
2) Importance that children have Japanese Americans as friends (4 point scale)	x=1.88	x=3.36	*t*=-8.19***
3) Importance that children date Japanese Americans (4 point scale)	x=1.36	x=3.36	*t*=-12.44***
4) Importance that children marry Japanese Americans (4 point scale)	x=1.64	x=3.20	*t*=-6.78***
5) Importance that children maintain ties with the ethnic community (4 point scale)	x=1.84	x=3.52	*t*=-8.85***
6) Importance that children know something about their heritage (4 point scale)	x=2.92	x=3.96	*t*=-5.12***
7) Importance that children know Japanese language (4 point scale)	x=1.76	x=3.04	*t*=-5.12***

*$p \leq .05$

**$p \leq .01$

***$p \leq .001$

TABLE 6

SUMMARY OF SIGNIFICANT DIFFERENCES
MISCELLANEOUS QUESTIONS

	Low Ethnics	High Ethnics	Test and significance
1) Importance of living in an area with other Japanese Americans (4 point scale)	x=1.68	x=3.08	t=-6.34***
2) Experienced or heard about discrimination in schools against Japanese Americans	28%	64%	X^2=4.649*
3) Extent to which feel hindered in American society because Japanese American (4 point scale)	x=1.48	x=2.04	t=-2.46**
4) Extent to which being Japanese American has been an advantage (4 point scale)	x=2.16	x=2.04	t=-2.34**
5) Believe that although caucasians may accept Japanese Americans in business dealings and work situations, in general they prefer not to mix with Japanese Americans socially	20%	44%	n.s.
6) Believe that although Japanese Americans may accpet caucasians in business dealings and work situations in general they prefer not to mix with caucasians socially.	48%	80%	X^2=4.253*

* $p \leq .05$

** $p \leq .01$

*** $p \leq .001$

APPENDIX B

JAPANESE AMERICAN ETHNICITY QUESTIONNAIRE

Japanese American Ethnicity Questionnaire

Principle Investigator: Kaoru Oguri Kendis
Department of Anthropology
University of Pittsburgh
Pittsburgh, Pennsylvania

Name:

Address:

Phone number:

Date:

Time begun:

Time ended:

Administered by:

Identification number: [ ]

		[1] 1
Identification number		[ ] 2-4
1. Age	[ ]	[ ] 5-6
2. Sex Male . . . . . . Female	 [1] [2]	[ ] 7
3. Generation Sansei . . . . . . Yonsei	 [1] [2]	[ ] 8
4. Marital Status Single . . . . . . Engaged or steady girl/boyfriend . . Married . . . . . Separated or divorced . . . . Widowed	 [1] [2] [3] [4] [5]	[ ] 9
5. Is (or was) your spouse, fiance, girl/boyfriend Japanese . . . . . Japanese American . . . . Caucasian . . . . . Other (specify)________ . Not applicable (no spouse, fiance, or steady girl/boyfriend) .	 [1] [2] [3] [4] [5]	[ ] 10
6. If your spouse, fiance, girl/boyfriend is Japanese American, is she/he Issei . . . . . . Kibei . . . . . . Nisei . . . . . . Sansei . . . . . . Yonsei . . . . . . (Not applicable) . .	 [1] [2] [3] [4] [5] [9]	[ ] 11

2

7. What is the highest level of education you have attained?

Elementary School	[01]	[ ]	12-13
Junior High School	[02]		
Some High School	[03]		
High School	[04]		
Business or Trade School . .	[05]		
Junior College or Some College (4 year) .	[06]		
Bachelors Degree . . .	[07]		
Masters Degree or Professional Equivalent .	[08]		
Professional Degree (Law, Medicine, Dentistry, etc.) .	[09]		
Ph.D., Post-doctorate	[10]		
Other (specify)________ .	[11]		

8. What is your present occupation (specify)?

________________ [ ] 14-15

9. Approximately what is your yearly income?

None	[01]	$20,000 - $24,999 . .	[06]	[ ]	16-17
Below $5,000	[02]	$25,000 - $29,999 . .	[07]		
$ 5,000 - $ 9,999 . .	[03]	$30,000 - $34,999 . .	[08]		
$10,000 - $14,999 . .	[04]	$35,000 - $39,999 . .	[09]		
$15,000 - $19,999 . .	[05]	$40,000 and above . .	[10]		

10. Approximately what is the yearly income of your spouse?

No spouse	[99]			[ ]	18-19
None	[01]	$20,000 - $24,999 . .	[06]		
Below $5,000	[02]	$25,000 - $29,999 . .	[07]		
$ 5,000 - $ 9,999 . .	[03]	$30,000 - $34,999 . .	[08]		
$10,000 - $14,999 . .	[04]	$35,000 - $39,999 . .	[09]		
$15,000 - $19,999 . .	[05]	$40,000 and above . .	[10]		

11. Do you consider yourself to be

Working Class	[1]	[ ]	20
Lower Middle Class .	[2]		
Middle Middle Class .	[3]		
Upper Middle Class .	[4]		
Upper Class	[5]		

3

12. How many children do you have? . . . [ ] | [ ] 21

Ages:
0 - 4 . . . [1]
5 - 12 . . . [2]
13 - 17 . . . [3]
18 - 21 . . . [4]
22 - up . . . [5]
N/A . . . [9]

Child 1 . . [ ] | [ ] 22
2 . . [ ] | [ ] 23
3 . . [ ] | [ ] 24
4 . . [ ] | [ ] 25
5 . . [ ] | [ ] 26
6 . . [ ] | [ ] 27
7 . . [ ] | [ ] 28
8 . . [ ] | [ ] 29

13. Were you ever in a relocation camp during World War II?

No . . [0]
Yes . . [1] | [ ] 30

If yes, at what age did you enter?. [ ] | [ ] 31-32
(N/A). [99]

14. Was your spouse, fiance, or girl/boyfriend ever in a relocation camp during World War II?

N/A . . [9] | [ ] 33
No . . [0]
Yes . . [1]

If yes, at what age did they enter?. [ ] | [ ] 34-35
(N/A). [99]

15. Was your father in a relocation camp during WW II?

No . . [0] | [ ] 36
Yes . . [1]

16. Was your mother in a relocation camp during WW II?

No . . [0] | [ ] 37
Yes . . [1]

4

17. Where were you born?

Los Angeles area . . [1]	Hawaii . . . . [5]	[ ] 38
Southern California . [2]	Other mainland U.S. . . [6]	
Northern California . [3]	Japan . . . . [7]	
Pacific Northwest . . [4]	Other foreign country . [8]	

18. Where were you raised as a child (specify)?

______________________ [ ] 39-43

19. Where do you presently reside (specify)?

______________________ [ ] 44-48

20. How many years have you lived in this area?

1 Year or Less . . [1]	11 - 15 Years . . . . . [4]	[ ] 49
2 - 5 Years . . . [2]	16 - 20 Years . . . . . [5]	
6 - 10 Years . . . [3]	More than 20 Years . . [6]	

21. Where did you live previously (specify)?

______________________ [ ] 50-54

22. How many Japanese and Japanese Americans would you estimate there are living in your neighborhood?

None . . . . . [1]	About 1/2 . . . . . [4]	[ ] 55
Very few . . . . . [2]	About 3/4 . . . . . [5]	
About 1/4 . . . . . [3]	All or nearly all . [6]	

23. On a 4 point scale how important is it to you that you live in an area where there are other Japanese Americans?

1 not important at all — 2 — 3 — 4 extremely important [ ] 56

5

24. What is your religious affiliation?

None . . . . [1] Christian . . . . [3]
Buddhist . . . . [2] Other (specify) . . . . [4] [ ] 57

25. What is the religious affiliation of your spouse?

Not applicable . [9] Christian . . . . [3]
None . . . . [1] Other (specify) . . . . [4] [ ] 58
Buddhist . . . . [2]

26. In what religion were you raised as a child?

None . . . . [1] Christian . . . . [3]
Buddhist . . . . [2] Other (specify) . . . . [4] [ ] 59

27. What is/was the religious affiliation of your father?

None . . . . [1] Christian . . . . [3]
Buddhist . . . . [2] Other (specify) . . . . [4] [ ] 60

28. What is/was the religious affiliation of your mother?

None . . . . [1] Christian . . . . [3]
Buddhist . . . . [2] Other (specify) . . . . [4] [ ] 61

29. How often do you attend church services?

N/A (non-believer or don't attend) [9]
Almost never . . . . . . [0]
Less than once a month . . . . . . [1] [ ] 62
Once a month . . . . . . [2]
Several times a month . . . . . . [3]
Once a week or more . . . . . . [4]

30. Is the minister of your church Japanese American or Japanese?

No . . . . [1] [ ] 63
Yes . . . . [2]
N/A . . . . [9]

6

31. Is the congregation in the church you go to

N/A, don't go to church . . . . [9]
Except for you, all or nearly all
non-Japanese American and non-Japanese . . . . [0]
Mainly non-Japanese American and non-Japanese . . [1]
Mixed (about 1/2 Japanese and Japanese American
and 1/2 non-Japanese and Japanese American) . . [2]
Mainly Japanese American and Japanese . . . . . . [3]
All or nearly all Japanese American and
Japanese . . . . [4]

[ ] 64

32. On a scale of 1 to 4 how important would you say that religion is to you?

1	2	3	4
not important at all			extremely important

[ ] 65

The next 7 questions deal with attitudes regarding your children. If you do not have children try to estimate how you would feel if you did.

33. On a 4 point scale how important is it to you that your children have Japanese Americans as friends?

1	2	3	4
not important at all			extremely important

[ ] 66

34. How important is it to you that your children date Japanese Americans?

1	2	3	4
not important at all			extremely important

[ ] 67

35. How important is it to you that your children marry Japanese Americans?

1	2	3	4
not important at all			extremely important

[ ] 68

7

36. How important is it to you that your children know something about their heritage?

1	2	3	4
not important at all			extremely important

[ ] 69

37. How important do you feel it is that your children know the Japanese language?

1	2	3	4
not important at all			extremely important

[ ] 70

38. How important is it to you that your children maintain some ties with the Japanese American community?

1	2	3	4
not important at all			extremely important

[ ] 71

39. How important to you is it that your children identify themselves as Japanese American?

1	2	3	4
not important at all			extremely important

[ ] 72

40. If a major newspaper were to insult the Japanese Americans, do you think you would feel insulted?

No . . . . [1]
Yes . . . . [2]

[ ] 73

41. If a major newspaper were to praise the Japanese Americans, do you think you would feel pleased?

No . . . . [1]
Yes . . . . [2]

[ ] 74

8

42. On a scale of 1 to 4 how much do you feel your fate is bound up with the fate of other Japanese Americans?

1	2	3	4	[ ] 75
not important at all			extremely important	

43. On a scale of 1 to 4 how much do you feel your fate is bound up with the fate of other Americans?

1	2	3	4	[ ] 76
not important at all			extremely important	

44. Below are 4 categories; put a 1 by the category that you feel best describes you, a 2 next to the category that is the second best descriptor, a 3 by the third best descriptor and a 4 next to the category which you feel describes you the poorest.

Japanese American . . . [ ] [ ] 77
Japanese . . . . [ ] [ ] 78
American . . . . [ ] [ ] 79
Asian American . . . . [ ] [ ] 80

[2] 1
ID # [ ] 2-4
Col. 77 - Col. 79: If +..[2]
If -..[1] [ ] 5

45. On a 4 point scale where do you feel you best fit?

1	2	3	4	[ ] 6
Americanness			Japaneseness	

46. Do you feel that you have become more Japanese or do more Japanese or Japanese American things as you have gotten older?

No . . . . [1] [ ] 7
Yes . . . . [2]

47. How important is it to you that some sort of Japanese identity continue to exist?

1	2	3	4	
not important at all			extremely important	[ ] 8

48. Speaking just for yourself, what do you feel the effect of Japanese Americans marrying Caucasians will be on the whole for Japanese Americans?

Good for Japanese Americans . . . . [1]
Balances out - both positive and negative aspects . . . . [2]
Bad for Japanese Americans . . . . [3]
Makes no difference . . . . [4]

[ ] 9

49. Would it bother you if Japanese Americans intermarried to such an extent that eventually there would no longer be any "pure" Japanese Americans?

1	2	3	4	
wouldn't bother you at all			would bother you a great deal	[ ] 10

50. How much does the fact of your being Japanese American influence things that you say or do?

Influences nothing . . . . [0]
Influences few things . . . . [1]
Influences some things . . . [2]
Influences many things . . . [3]
Influences nearly everything . . . [4]

[ ] 11

51. On what occasions do you feel more Japanese (or Japanese American)? Check as many as are applicable.

No . . . [0]
Yes . . . [1]

No occasion . . . [ ] [ ] 12
When you are with other Japanese or Japanese Americans . . . [ ] [ ] 13
When you are with non-Japanese Americans or non-Japanese . . . [ ] [ ] 14

10

Religious occasions . .	[ ]	[ ]	15
Japanese cultural events .	[ ]	[ ]	16
Political events . .	[ ]	[ ]	17
Occupation . . .	[ ]	[ ]	18
Recreational, social events .	[ ]	[ ]	19
Family occasions . .	[ ]	[ ]	20
Organizational meetings .	[ ]	[ ]	21
In unfamiliar cities or situations . . .	[ ]	[ ]	22

Total col. 13 - 22:

0	[0]		
1-2	[1]		
3-4	[2]		
5-6	[3]	[ ]	23
7-8	[4]		
9-10. . . .	[5]		

52. On a scale of 1 to 4 do you feel you are more American or Japanese American/Japanese in your outlook on life?

1 American 2 3 4 Japanese American/ Japanese [ ] 24

53. On a scale of 1 to 4 do you feel you are more American or Japanese American/Japanese in the values and beliefs you have?

1 American 2 3 4 Japanese American/ Japanese [ ] 25

54. On a scale of 1 to 4 do you feel you are more American or Japanese American/Japanese in your way of relating to people?

1 American 2 3 4 Japanese American/ Japanese [ ] 26

55. On a scale of 1 to 4 do you feel you are more American or Japanese American/Japanese in the way you are or would wish to raise your children?

1	2	3	4
American			Japanese American/ Japanese

[ ] 27

56. On a scale of 1 to 4 how important a part does the fact that you are Japanese American play in your life?

1	2	3	4
no part at all			very important part

[ ] 28

57. Do you feel more comfortable with Japanese Americans or with non-Japanese Americans?

Much more comfortable with non-Japanese Americans . [1]
Somewhat more comfortable with non-Japanese Americans . . . . [2]
Makes no difference . . . . . . [3]
Somewhat more comfortable with Japanese Americans . [4]
Much more comfortable with Japanese Americans . [5]

[ ] 29

58. Do you feel closer to people of Japanese ancestry than to persons of any other background?

No, makes no difference . . . . [1]
Yes . . . . [2]

[ ] 30

59. To what extent do you feel you have been hindered in American society because you are Japanese American?

1	2	3	4
not hindered at all			very badly hindered

[ ] 31

60. To what extent do you feel being Japanese American has been an advantage?

1	2	3	4
made no difference			was an extreme help

[ ] 32

Below is a list of some ways in which discrimination against Japanese Americans is said to have occurred. Will you please try to remember whether in the past 10 years or so you or your immediate family have experienced any of these forms of discrimination personally? Next, for any of these forms of discrimination would you please try to remember if you have heard about cases in which other Japanese Americans experienced it in the past 10 years?

Discrimination in:	Experienced Personally	Heard About	Neither Experienced nor Heard About		
61. Housing	[2]	[1]	[0]	[ ]	33
62. Schools	[2]	[1]	[0]	[ ]	34
63. Jobs	[2]	[1]	[0]	[ ]	35
64. Personal life	[2]	[1]	[0]	[ ]	36
65. Police brutality	[2]	[1]	[0]	[ ]	37

66. Would you agree or disagree with the following statement? Although Caucasians may accept Japanese Americans in business dealings and work situations, in general they prefer not to mix with Japanese Americans socially.

Agree . . . . . [2]
Disagree . . . . [1]

[ ] 38

67. Would you agree or disagree with the following statement? Although Japanese Americans may accept Caucasians in business dealings and work situations, in general they prefer not to mix with Caucasians socially.

Agree . . . . . [2]
Disagree . . . . [1]

[ ] 39

68. In general how do you feel Caucasian parents would react if the person their child wanted to marry was Japanese American?

Have reservations . . . . . [1]
Her/his being Japanese American wouldn't make a difference . . . . . [2]
Pleased because she/he is Japanese American . [3]

[ ] 40

69. Thinking back over your dating years from high school age and up, generally speaking, did you date

All Japanese and Japanese Americans . . [4]
Mostly Japanese and Japanese Americans . [3]
About 1/2 Japanese/Japanese Americans and 1/2 non-Japanese/Japanese Americans . [2]
Mostly non-Japanese/Japanese Americans . [1]
All non-Japanese/Japanese Americans . . [0]

[ ] 41

70. You are being asked to contribute to a charitable cause. Will you be more likely to make a contribution if the person asking is Japanese American?

No . . . . [1]
Yes . . . . [2]

[ ] 42

71. Will you be more likely to make a contribution if the cause is specifically aimed at aiding Japanese Americans as opposed to one that is aimed at aiding people regardless of background?

No . . . . [1]
Yes . . . . [2]

[ ] 43

72. What percent of your yearly contributions go to Japanese American/Japanese organizations or causes?

None . . . . [1]
1 - 33% . [2]
34 - 66% . [3]
67 - 100% . [4]

[ ] 44

73. Would you be more likely to vote for a political candidate if he/she were Japanese American?

1 makes no difference 2 3 4 much more likely

[ ] 45

74. Would you be more willing to use your influence to help a Japanese American get a job than if he/she were not Japanese American?

1 makes no difference 2 3 4 much more likely

[ ] 46

75. Is your doctor Japanese American (or Japanese)?

No . . . . [1]
Yes . . . . [2]
Have none . [9]

[ ] 47

76. Is your dentist Japanese American (or Japanese)?

No . . . . [1]
Yes . . . . [2]
Have none . [9]

[ ] 48

77. Is your optometrist Japanese American (or Japanese)?

No . . . . [1]
Yes . . . . [2]
Have none . [9]

[ ] 49

78. Is your lawyer Japanese American (or Japanese)?

No . . . . [1]
Yes . . . . [2]
Have none . [9]

[ ] 50

79. Is your insurance agent Japanese American (or Japanese)?

No . . . . [1]
Yes . . . . [2]
Have none . [9]

[ ] 51

30. Do you bank at a Japan based bank?

No . . . . [1]
Yes . . . . [2]
Have none . [9]

[ ] 52

31. Do you subscribe to any Japanese or Japanese American periodicals or newspapers?

No . . . . [1]
Yes . . . . [2]

[ ] 53

82. How well do you know the Japanese language?

Do not know the language at all . . . . . [1]
Can understand a few words . . . . . . [2]
Can understand it and use a few expressions . [3]
Can speak and understand it . . . . . . [4]

[ ] 54

83. Where did you learn Japanese? Select the answer that you feel contributed the most.

Home . . . . [1]
Japanese Language School . . . . . [2]
Public School or College . . . . . [3]
Friends . . . . [4]
Other (specify) ________________ . [5]
N/A - never learned Japanese . . . [9]

[ ] 55

84. Do you speak Japanese or use Japanese expressions and words in your speech at home or with your family?

No . . [1]
Yes . [2]

[ ] 56

85. Do you speak Japanese or use Japanese expressions and words when you're with your friends?

No . . [1]
Yes . [2]

[ ] 57

86. Do you speak Japanese or use Japanese expressions and words where you work?

No . . [1]
Yes . [2]

[ ] 58

87. Is your circle of friends

Except for you, all nonJapanese American/Japanese . [0]
Mainly nonJapanese American/Japanese . . . . [1]
About ½ Japanese American/Japanese . . . . [2]
Mainly Japanese American/Japanese . . . . [3]
All Japanese American/Japanese . . . . [4]

[ ] 59

16

88. How many of your close friends are Japanese American?

All . . . . . . [4] Few . . . . . . [1]
Most . . . . . . [3] None . . . . . . [0]
About half . . . [2]

[ ] 60

89. How many of your other friends are Japanese American?

All . . . . . . [4] Few . . . . . . [1]
Most . . . . . . [3] None . . . . . . [0]
About half . . . [2]

[ ] 61

90. Do you have one main group of friends who seem to do most of their socializing together or do you socialize with different groups according to the activity?

Different groups . [1]
Same group . . . . [2]

[ ] 62

91. How important is it to you that you associate with other Japanese Americans?

1 2 3 4
not important at all — extremely important

[ ] 63

92. In your job how many of your co-workers are Japanese American or Japanese?

Nearly all . . [4] None . . . . [0]
More than ½ . . [3] N/A - no co-workers . [9]
About ½ . . . . [2] or not employed
Less than ½ . . [1]

[ ] 64

93. In your job how many of your clients are Japanese American or Japanese?

Nearly all . . [4] None . . . . [0]
More than ½ . . [3] N/A - no clients . . [9]
About ½ . . . . [2] or not employed
Less than ½ . . [1]

[ ] 65

17

94. What business or professional organizations do you belong to? What percent of the membership do Japanese Americans and Japanese make up in each organization?

	Less than 50%	About 50% or more	
a. ______	[0]	[1]	[ ] 66
b. ______	[0]	[1]	[ ] 67
c. ______	[0]	[1]	[ ] 68
d. ______	[0]	[1]	[ ] 69
e. ______	[0]	[1]	[ ] 70
f. ______	[0]	[1]	[ ] 71
g. ______	[0]	[1]	[ ] 72
h. ______	[0]	[1]	[ ] 73

Total col. 66 - 73:
1 - 2 . . . [1]
3 - 4 . . . [2]
5 - 6 . . . [3]
7 - 8 . . . [4]
[ ] 74

[3] 1
ID # [ ] 2-4

95. What service and community organizations do you belong to? What percent of the membership do Japanese Americans and Japanese make up in each organization?

	Less than 50%	About 50% or more	
a. ______	[0]	[1]	[ ] 5
b. ______	[0]	[1]	[ ] 6
c. ______	[0]	[1]	[ ] 7
d. ______	[0]	[1]	[ ] 8
e. ______	[0]	[1]	[ ] 9
f. ______	[0]	[1]	[ ] 10
g. ______	[0]	[1]	[ ] 11
h. ______	[0]	[1]	[ ] 12

Total col. 5 - 12:
1 - 2 . . . [1]
3 - 4 . . . [2]
5 - 6 . . . [3]
7 - 8 . . . [4]

[ ] 13

96. What social organizations, hobby clubs, and athletic clubs do you belong to? What percent of the membership do Japanese Americans and Japanese make up in each organization?

	Less than 50%	About 50% or more	
a. ____________	[0]	[1]	[ ] 14
b. ____________	[0]	[1]	[ ] 15
c. ____________	[0]	[1]	[ ] 16
d. ____________	[0]	[1]	[ ] 17
e. ____________	[0]	[1]	[ ] 18
f. ____________	[0]	[1]	[ ] 19
g. ____________	[0]	[1]	[ ] 20
h. ____________	[0]	[1]	[ ] 21

Total col. 14 - 21:
1 - 2 . . . [1]
3 - 4 . . . [2]
5 - 6 . . . [3]
7 - 8 . . . [4]

[ ] 22

97. What political organizations do you belong to? What percent of the membership do Japanese Americans and Japanese make up in each organization?

	Less than 50%	About 50% or more	
a. ____________	[0]	[1]	[ ] 23
b. ____________	[0]	[1]	[ ] 24
c. ____________	[0]	[1]	[ ] 25
d. ____________	[0]	[1]	[ ] 26
e. ____________	[0]	[1]	[ ] 27

19

f.	______________	[0]	[1]	[ ] 28
g.	______________	[0]	[1]	[ ] 29
h.	______________	[0]	[1]	[ ] 30

Total col. 23 - 30:
1 - 2 . . . [1]
3 - 4 . . . [2]
5 - 6 . . . [3]
7 - 8 . . . [4]

[ ] 31

98. What religious organizations do you belong to? What percent of the membership do Japanese Americans and Japanese make up in each organization?

		Less than 50%	About 50% or more	
a.	______________	[0]	[1]	[ ] 32
b.	______________	[0]	[1]	[ ] 33
c.	______________	[0]	[1]	[ ] 34
d.	______________	[0]	[1]	[ ] 35
e.	______________	[0]	[1]	[ ] 36
f.	______________	[0]	[1]	[ ] 37
g.	______________	[0]	[1]	[ ] 38
h.	______________	[0]	[1]	[ ] 39

Total col. 32 - 39:
1 - 2 . . . [1]
3 - 4 . . . [2]
5 - 6 . . . [3]
7 - 8 . . . [4]

[ ] 40

99. What other organizations not listed previously do you belong to? What percent of the membership do Japanese Americans and Japanese make up in each organization?

		Less than 50%	About 50% or more	
a.	______________	[0]	[1]	[ ] 41
b.	______________	[0]	[1]	[ ] 42

c. ______________________________ [0] [1] [ ] 43
d. ______________________________ [0] [1] [ ] 44
e. ______________________________ [0] [1] [ ] 45
f. ______________________________ [0] [1] [ ] 46
g. ______________________________ [0] [1] [ ] 47
h. ______________________________ [0] [1] [ ] 48

Total col. 41 - 48:
1 - 2 . . . [1]
3 - 4 . . . [2] [ ] 49
5 - 6 . . . [3]
7 - 8 . . . [4]

100. While growing up how much formal training or instruction did you have in Japanese culture? Indicate on a scale of 1 to 4.

1 none 2 3 4 a great deal [ ] 50

101. How often do you attend or take part in:

a. Obon festival - dance and/or carnival

Often (every year or several times a year) . [4]
Occasionally (every few years) . . . . [3] [ ] 51
A few times (2 or 3) . . . . [2]
Once or never . . . . [1]

b. Nisei Week Activities

Often (every year) . . . . [4]
Occasionally (every few years) . . . . [3] [ ] 52
A few times (2 or 3) . . . . [2]
Once or never . . . . [1]

c. Carnivals given by Japanese American organizations

Often (several times a year) . . . . [4]
Once a year . . . . [3] [ ] 53
Occasionally (every few years) . . . . [2]
Never or once or twice . . . . [1]

d. Dinners (fund raising, testimonial, ceremonial, etc.) given by Japanese American or Japanese organizations

Often (several times a year)	[4]	[ ] 54
Once a year	[3]	
Occasionally (every few years) . . .	[2]	
Never or once or twice	[1]	

e. Social dances given by Japanese American or Japanese organizations

Often (several times a year)	[4]	[ ] 55
Once a year	[3]	
Occasionally (every few years) . . .	[2]	
Never or once or twice	[1]	

f. Sports tournaments and games given by or involving Japanese American or Japanese organizations

Often (several times a year)	[4]	[ ] 56
Once a year	[3]	
Every few years	[2]	
Never or once or twice	[1]	

g. Entertainment shows, demonstrations, exhibitions given by or involving Japanese American or Japanese organizations or pertaining to Japanese culture

Often (several times a year)	[4]	[ ] 57
Once a year	[3]	
Every few years	[2]	
Never or once or twice	[1]	

h. Educational talks, lectures given by Japanese American or Japanese organizations or directed towards Japanese Americans and Japanese American concerns

Often (several times a year)	[4]	[ ] 58
Once a year	[3]	
Every few years	[2]	
Never or once or twice	[1]	

22

i. Picnics, beach parties, one day excursions given by Japanese American or Japanese organizations

Often (several times a year) . . . . . . [4]
Once a year . . . . [3]
Every few years . . . . [2]
Never or once or twice . . . . [1]

[ ] 59

j. Trips (more than 1 day - e.g., camping, skiing, travel to other states and countries, etc.) given by Japanese American or Japanese organizations

Often (yearly) . . . . [4]
Occasionally (once every few years) . . . [3]
A few times (2 or 3) . . . . [2]
Once or never . . . . [1]

[ ] 60

k. Informal social dinners, parties, get-togethers given by Japanese American or Japanese organizations or individuals or involving Japanese American or Japanese guests

Often (several times a year) . . . . . . [4]
Once a year . . . . [3]
Every few years . . . . [2]
Never or once or twice . . . . [1]

[ ] 61

Do you agree or disagree with the following statements.

101. One must behave properly to avoid bringing shame to one's family.

Agree . . . . . [2]
Disagree . . . [1]

[ ] 62

102. To lose a competition is to be disgraced.

Agree . . . . . [2]
Disagree . . . [1]

[ ] 63

103. One must make returns for all kindnesses received.

Agree . . . . . [2]
Disagree . . . [1]

[ ] 64

104. One must act so as not to bring dishonor to the Japanese American community.

Agree . . . . . [2]
Disagree . . . [1]

[ ] 65

NOTES

METHODOLOGY

1. In each case as close as possible to 25% from the top and bottom were selected, with the condition that none constitute less than 20% of the total sample. Actual percentages ranged from a low of 20.6% to a high of 28.4% and averaged 25.2%.

2. For interval level data Pearson product moment correlation coefficients were computed for each item with the total category score excluding that item, and those items which discriminated between high and low scorers at the $p \leq .05$ level were retained. Of the 40 interval level items retained 37 reached a significance level of $p \leq .001$. For nominal and ordinal level data, chi square values were computed and all such items retained reached a significance level of $p \leq .005$.

DIFFERENCES BETWEEN HIGH AND LOW ETHNICS

1. Education was defined as the highest level the individual had attained. Everyone in the sample had a high school education or better and most people had a bachelor's degree or better (low ethnics - 60%, high ethnics - 76%).

2. Occupations were classified into five categories:

Category 1: Housewife, part-time worker, unemployed
Category 2: Manual or unskilled, drivers, salesclerks
Category 3: Trade or crafts, clerical, low level office worker, sales representative, service personnel, preschool teacher
Category 4: Small business owner (usually a one man operation), low level professional (teacher, nurse, counselor, accountant, etc.), supervisory, low level management, scientist or engineer with B.S. or M.S. degree
Category 5: Professional (doctor, dentist, lawyer, etc.), mid-size business owner, mid- to high-level management, Ph.D., architect.

Two tests were made. In the first test the individual's own occupation was used. In the second, if the individual was married the higher level category of the couple was used. In neither case was there a significant difference between the high ethnics and the low ethnics.

3. Here income is the estimated household income which was computed by taking the midpoints of the income categories of the informant and spouse and summing the two.

4. Tables summarizing significant differences are presented in Appendix A.

5. A variety of different statistical tests were applied to the data, depending upon the level of measurement. In all cases in order to be considered "significant" the probability of the strength of the relationship occurring by chance had to reach a level of $p \leq .05$. All differences cited in this chapter were significant unless otherwise specified.

WHY DOES ETHNICITY PERSIST FOR LATER GENERATIONS?

1. In a study done on *kibei* (second-generation Japanese Americans who had been born in America but raised and educated in Japan for a period of years during their childhood before returning to America) and *nisei* (second-generation Japanese Americans raised and educated in America) who had renounced their American citizenship and returned to Japan after World War II, Gladys Ishida found that after 8 years of residence in Japan the *nisei* still were finding it difficult to adjust. They were ridiculed by the Japanese for their lack of proficiency in Japanese, their lack of proper Japanese manners, and their display of American patterns of behavior, even though to these American-born and raised *nisei* Japan was as foreign to them as America was to their parents. Consequently they have modified their behavior only to the point that it will enable them to obtain employment and prevent conflict with their parents. Aside from that as much as they are able to and can afford it they attempt to recreate a Western way of life and, particularly in the urban areas, seek to congregate with other *nisei* (Ishida 1955).

2. Until this was pointed out to me I unintentionally caused some amount of embarrassment to some Japanese Americans. I had asked people if they would mind answering a questionnaire. For those who didn't mind, my stating the request in this fashion caused no difficulties and I probably also was able to obtain agreement from others because of their inability to say "no, I would mind" and by doing so, embarrass me and themselves. However, there were others who didn't want to say yes, and yet found it impossible to say no, given the wording of my request and given the rules of behavior they followed. They would go into long elaborate explanations of how busy they were while under the pretense of trying to find time to see me until even I eventually realized that they were "too busy" to see me in the foreseeable future even though they "wanted to." When I then offered the excuse "You seem too busy right now. Why don't I try some other time?" it was eagerly accepted. The interchange was then terminated with the unspoken understanding that I would not call again and thus, both of our feelings were spared according to Japanese American rules of behavior. An alternate strategy was to agree initially but to continually cancel the appointments because of some forgotten prior commitment.

3. Many of these cultural differences probably have their origins in the Japanese culture of the *Meiji* era that their grandparents, the *issei*, brought with them to America. However, with the different stresses and influences encountered in a new culture what was once Japanese has over the generations evolved to become something more unique to the Japanese Americans.

HOW IS ETHNICITY MAINTAINED?

1. Kurokawa (1972) found in a study she conducted in California on acculturation and rates of childhood accidents that children of oriental ancestry had fewer injuries than did caucasian or black American children - one out of every 3.7 caucasian children went to the hospital for treatment versus one out of every 6.7 oriental

children. Her study also found that it is the mother with the more permissive attitude towards her child's risk-taking who is more likely to have a high accident rate child which is, in essence, what the *sansei* mothers complain about. Kurokawa, however, also feels that accident rates will rise with increasing acculturation.

2. Japanese Americans often remarked that they take more care in selecting a wedding gift for Japanese Americans than nonJapanese Americans. This is probably due in part to the gift opening ceremony since they know that other members of the ethnic community will be seeing the gifts and will know who the givers are.

3. Of the total sample of 102, 76.5% agreed with the statement that "One must make returns for all kindnesses received." Many of the 23.5% who disagreed with this statement disagreed because of the word "must." They felt, instead, "one should if one can." Even when analyzing the smaller sample of 50 high and low ethnics there was a 76% agreement with this statement (92% of the high ethnics and 60% of the low ethnics).

BIBLIOGRAPHY

Arkoff, Abe
1959 Need Patterns in Two Generations of Japanese Americans in Hawaii. The Journal of Social Psychology 50:75-79.

Barth, Fredrik
1969 Introduction. In Ethnic Groups and Boundaries: The Social Organization of Culture Difference. Fredrik Barth, ed. Pp. 9-38. Boston: Little, Brown and Co.

Befu, Harumi
1974 Gift-Giving in a Modernizing Japan. In Japanese Culture and Behavior. Takie Sugiyama Lebra and William P. Lebra, eds. Pp. 208-221. Honolulu: University Press of Hawaii.

Berreman, Gerald
1975 Bazaar Behavior: Social Identity and Social Interaction in Urban India. In Cultural Continuities and Change. George De Vos and Lola Romanucci-Ross, eds. Pp. 74-105. Palo Alto: Mayfield Publishing Co.

Blom, Jan-Petter
1969 Ethnic and Cultural Differentiation. In Ethnic Groups and Boundaries: The Social Organization of Culture Difference. Fredrik Barth, ed. Pp. 74-85. Boston: Little, Brown, and Co.

Broom, Leonard and John I. Kitsuse
1956 The Managed Casualty - The Japanese-American Family in World War II. Berkeley: University of California Press.

Caudill, William
1952 Japanese-American Personality and Acculturation. Genetic Psychology Monographs 45:3-102.

Caudill, William and George De Vos
1956 Achievement, Culture and Personality: The Case of the Japanese Americans. American Anthropologist 58:1102-1126.

City of Gardena Community Development Department
1978 1978 Gardena Special Census: Summary of City-Wide Results.

Cohen, Abner
1974 The Lesson of Ethnicity. In Urban Ethnicity. Abner Cohen, ed. Pp. ix-xxiv. New York: Tavistock Publications.

Connor, John
1976 Value Continuities and Change in Three Generations of Japanese Americans. Ethos 4:232-264.

Corrado, Raymond R.
1975a Ethnicity: A Conceptual Definition and Typology with an Empirical Assessment in Wales. Working paper No. 31. Comparative Interdisciplinary Studies Section of the International Studies Association: University of Pittsburgh.

1975b Nationalism and Communalism in Wales. Ethnicity 2:360-381.

Daniels, Roger
1972 Japanese Immigrants on a Western Frontier: The Issei in California, 1890-1940. In East Across the Pacific. Francis Hilary Conroy and T. Scott Miyakawa, eds. Pp. 76-91. Santa Barbara: American Bibliographical-Clio Press.

De Vos, George
1975 Ethnic Pluralism: Conflict and Accommodation. In Ethnic Identity: Cultural Continuities and Change. George De Vos and Lola Romanucci-Ross, eds. Pp. 5-41. Palo Alto: Mayfield Publishing Co.

Despres, Leo A.
1975 Toward a Theory of Ethnic Phenomena. In Ethnicity and Resource Competition in Plural Societies. Leo A. Despres, ed. Pp. 187-207. Paris: Mouton Publishers.

Dirks, Robert
1975 Ethnicity and Ethnic Group Relations in the British Virgin Islands. In The New Ethnicity: Perspectives from Ethnology. John W. Bennett, ed. Pp. 95-109. St. Paul: West Publishing Co.

Ebuchi, Kazukimi
1971 The Meaning of "Ethnic" Identity to Burakumin Children: A Case Study of an Urban Neighborhood in Northern Kyushu, Japan. Revised and enlarged version of paper presented at the Council on Anthropology and Education Symposium "Ethnicity and Education," New York, 1971.

Feagin, Joe R. and Nancy Fujitaki
1972 On the Assimilation of Japanese Americans. Amerasia Journal 1(4):13-30.

Francis, E. K.
1976 Interethnic Relations: An Essay in Sociological Theory. New York: Elsevier Scientific Publishing Co.

Gaines, Donald W.
1976 Social Profile for the Gardena Community. Prepared for United Way Region III.

Glazer, Nathan and Daniel P. Moynihan
1970 Beyond the Melting Pot. Second ed. Cambridge: MIT Press.

Greer, Colin
1974 Remembering Class. In Divided Society: The Ethnic Experience in America. Colin Greer, ed. New York: Basic Books.

Hosokawa, Fumiko
1973 Social Interaction and Ethnic Identification Among the Third Generation Japanese. Ph.D. dissertation, Sociology Department, University of California at Los Angeles.

Ichihashi, Yamato
1932 Japanese in the U.S.: A Critical Study of the Problems of the Japanese Immigrants and their Children. Stanford: Stanford University Press.

Ishida, Gladys
1955 The Japanese American Renunciants of Okayama Prefecture: Their Accommodation and Assimilation to Japanese Culture. Ph.D. dissertation, University of Michigan.

Johnson, Colleen Leahy
1974 Gift Giving and Reciprocity Among the Japanese Americans in Honolulu. American Ethnologist 1:295-308.

Kagiwada, George
1969 Ethnic Identification and Socio-Economic Status: The Case of the Japanese Americans in Los Angeles. Ph.D. dissertation, Sociology Department, University of California at Los Angeles.

Kikumura, Akemi and Harry H. L. Kitano
1973 Interracial Marriage: A Picture of the Japanese Americans. Journal of Social Issues 29(2):67-81.

Kitano, Harry H. L.
1961 Differential Child-Rearing Attitudes between First and Second Generation Japanese in the United States. The Journal of Social Psychology 53:13-19.

1962 Changing Achievement Patterns of the Japanese in the United States. The Journal of Social Psychology 58:257-264.

1969 Japanese Americans: The Evolution of a Subculture. Englewood Cliffs: Prentice-Hall.

Kurokawa, Minako
1972 Acculturation and Childhood Accidents. In East Across the Pacific. Francis Hilary Conroy and T. Scott Miyakawa, eds. Pp. 244- 267. Santa Barbara: American Bibliographical-Clio Press.

Levine, Gene N. and Darrell M. Montero
1973 Socioeconomic Mobility among Three Generations of Japanese Americans. Journal of Social Issues 29(2):33-48.

Levy, Sydelle Brooks
1975 Shifting Patterns of Ethnic Identification among the Hassidim. In The New Ethnicity: Perspectives from Ethnology. John W. Bennett, ed. St. Paul: West Publishing Co.

Masuda, Minoru, Gary H. Matsumoto, and Gerald M. Meredith
1970 Ethnic Identity in Three Generations of Japanese Americans. The Journal of Social Psychology 8:119-207.

Maykovich, Minako K.
1972 Japanese American Identity Dilemma. Tokyo: Waseda University Press.

1973 Political Activation of Japanese American Youth. Journal of Social Issues 29(2):167-185.

Miyamoto, S. Frank
1972 An Immigrant Community in America. In East Across the Pacific. Francis Hilary Conroy and T. Scott Miyakawa, eds. Pp. 218-242. Santa Barbara: American Bibliographical-Clio Press.

Nagata, Judith
1974 What is a Malay? Situational Selection of Ethnic Identity in a Plural Society. In American Ethnologist 1:331-350.

Patterson, G. James
1979 A Critique of "The New Ethnicity." American Anthropologist 81:103-105.

Patterson, Orlando
1975 Context and Choice in Ethnic Allegiance: A Theoretical Framework and Caribbean Case Study. In Ethnicity: Theory and Experience. Nathan Glazer and Daniel P. Moynihan, eds. Pp. 305-349. Cambridge: Harvard University Press.

Schildkrout, Enid
1974 Ethnicity and Generational Differences among Urban Immigrants in Ghana. In Urban Ethnicity. Abner Cohen, ed. Pp. 187-222. New York: Tavistock Publications.

Schmid, Calvin F. and Charles E. Nobbe
1965 Socioeconomic Differentials among Nonwhite Races. American Sociological Review 30:909-922.

Schwartz, Audrey James
1971 The Culturally Advantaged: A Study of Japanese-American Pupils. Sociology and Social Research 55:341-353.

Soo Hoo, Stan
1974 Environmental Impact Report for the Housing Element of the General Plan. Community Development Department, Planning Division.

Thomas, Dorothy Swaine
1952 The Salvage: Japanese American Evacuation and Resettlement. Berkeley: University of California Press.

Tinker, John N.
1973 Intermarriage and Ethnic Boundaries: The Japanese-American Case. Journal of Social Issues 29(2):49-66.

INDEX

IMMIGRANT COMMUNITIES & ETHNIC MINORITIES IN THE UNITED STATES & CANADA: *continued*

31. Barbara L. Reimensnyder. *Powwowing in Union County: A Study of Pennsylvania German Folk Medicine in Context.*
32. Kaoru Oguri Kendis. *A Matter of Comfort: Ethnic Maintenance and Ethnic Style Among Third-Generation Japanese Americans.*
33. Randall Jay Kendis. *An Attitude of Gratitude: The Adaptation to Aging of the Elderly Japanese in America.*
34. Wesley R. Hurt. *Manzano: A Study of Community Disorganization.*
35. Chava Weissler. *Making Judaism Meaningful: Ambivalence and Tradition in a Havurah Community.*
36. Carolyn Stickney Beck. *Our Own Vine and Fig Tree: The persistence of the Mother Bethel Family.*
37. Charles C. Muzny. *The Vietnamese in Oklahoma City: A Study of Ethnic Change.*
38. Sathi Dasgupta. *On the Trail of an Uncertain Dream: Indian Immigrant Experience in America.*
39. Deborah Padgett. *Settlers and Sojourners: A Study of Serbian Adaptation in Milwaukee, Wisconsin.*
40. Margaret S. Boone. *Capital Cubans: Refugee Adaption in Washington, D.C.*
41. George James Patterson, Jr. *The Unassimilated Greeks of Denver.*
42. Mark M. Stolarik. *Immigration and Urbanization: The Slovak Experience.*
43. Dorita Sewell. *Knowing People: A Mexican-American Community's Concept of a person.*
44. M. Ann Walko. *Rejecting the Second Generation Hypothesis: Maintaining Estonian Ethnicity in Lakewood, New Jersey.*
45. Peter D. Goldsmith. *When I Rise Cryin' Holy: Afro-American Denominationalism on the Georgia Coast.*
46. Emily Bradley Massara. *Qué Gordita!: A Study of Weight Among Women in a Puerto Rican Community.*
47. Stephen L. Cabral. *Tradition and Transformation: Portuguese Feasting in New Bedford.*
48. Usha R. Jain. *The Gujaratis of San Francisco.*
49. Aleksandras Gedemintas. *An Interesting Bit of Identity: The Dynamics of Ethnic Identity in a Lithuanian-American Community.*
50. Suzanne J. Terrel. *This Other Kind of Doctors: Traditional Medical Systems in Black Neighborhoods in Austin, Texas.*
51. Annamma Joy. *Ethnicity in Canada: Social Accomodation and Cultural Persistence Among the Sikhs and the Portuguese.*
52. Maria Andrea Miralles. *A Matter of Life and Death: Health-seeking Behavior of Guatemalan Refugees in South Florida.*
53. Greta E. Swenson. *Festivals of Sharing: Family Reunions in America.*
54. Tekle Mariam Woldemikael. *Becoming Black American: Haitians and American Institutions in Evanston, Illinois.*
55. Louis James Cononelos. *In Search of Gold Paved Streets: Greek Immigrant Labor in the Far West, 1900—1920.*
56. Terry J. Prewitt. *German-American Settlement in an Oklahoma Town: Ecologic, Ethnic and Cultural Change.*
57. Myrna Silverman. *Strategies for Social Mobility: Family, Kinship and Ethnicity within Jewish Families in Pittsburgh.*
58. Peter Vasiliadis. *Whose Are You?: Identity and Ethnicity Among the Toronto Macedonians.*
59. Iftikhar Haider Malik. *Pakistanis in Michigan: A Study of Third Culture and Acculturation.*
60. Koozma J. Tarasoff. *Spells, Splits, and Survival in a Russian Canadian Community: A Study of Russian Organizations in the Greater Vancouver Area*
61. Alice H. Reich. *The Cultural Construction of Ethnicity: Chicanos in the University.*
62. Greta Kwik. *The Indos in Southern California.*
63. Laurence Marshall Carucci, et al. *Shared Spaces: Contexts of Interaction in Chicago's Ethnic Communities.*
64. Francis W. Chapin. *Tides of Migration: A Study of Migration Decision-Making and Social Progress in São Miguel, Azores.*
65. Robert B. Klymasz. *The Ukrainian Folk Ballad in Canada. With Musical Transcriptions by Kenneth Peacock.*
66. Elaine H. Maas. *The Jews of Houston: An Ethnographic Study.*
67. James W. Kiriazis. *Children of the Colossus: The Rhodian Greek Immigrants in the United States.*